OCR HISTORY B

Historical Controversies and Historical Significance

Mike Dickenson, Stephen Nutt, Andrew Pickering, Allan Todd and Andrew Watson | Series editor: Martin D W Jones

www.heinemann.co.uk

✓ Free online support
✓ Useful weblinks
✓ 24 hour online ordering

01865 888080

RECOGNISING ACHIEVEMENT

Official Publisher Partnership

Heinemann is an imprint of Pearson Education Limited, a company incorporated in England and Wales, having its registered office at Edinburgh Gate, Harlow, Essex, CM20 2JE. Registered company number: 872828

www.heinemann.co.uk

Heinemann is a registered trademark of Pearson Education Limited

Text © Pearson Education Limited 2009

First published 2009

13 12 11 10 09

10 9 8 7 6 5 4 3 2 1

British Library Cataloguing in Publication Data

A catalogue record for this book is available from the British Library

ISBN 978-0435312466

Copyright notice

Edited by Susan Ross
Typeset by Saxon Graphics Ltd, Derby
Original illustrations © Pearson Education Limited 2009
Illustrated by Saxon Graphics Ltd, Derby
Picture research by Zooid Pictures Limited
Cover photo/illustration: British poster © The Imperial War Museum; American and Soviet Union posters © Corbis
Printed in Spain by Graficas Estella

Acknowledgements
We would like to thank the Holocaust Education Trust for their invaluable help in the development of this course.

The authors and publisher would like to thank the following individuals and organisations for permission to reproduce photographs:

p. 3: © Rex Features/Nils Jorgenssen; p. 66: © Alamy/Mary Evans Picture Library; p. 70: © David King Collection; p. 88: © Bridgeman Art Library/British Library; p. 96: © Alamy/ INTERFOTO Pressebildagentur; p. 97: © akg-images; p. 105: © Bridgeman Art Library/Peter Newark American Pictures; p. 116: © Imperial War Museum; p. 117: © akg-images

Websites
There are links to relevant websites in this book. In order to ensure that the links are up to date, that the links work, and that the sites are not inadvertently linked to sites that could be considered offensive, we have made the links available on the Heinemann website at www.heinemann.co.uk/hotlinks. When you access the site, the express code is 2466P.

Contents

Notes for teachers

This book, *Historical Controversies and Historical Significance,* is designed to support OCR's History B specification. The first four chapters support Historical Controversies (F985/F986) and build upon Units F981/F982 and Units F983/F984 and examine how and why historians disagree about the past. Chapter 3 examines the four British history topics in Unit F985 and chapter 4 comprises four case studies based upon the non-British topics in Unit F986. At the end of both these chapters there is detailed exam preparation and support in the Exam Café, with further support materials on the CD-ROM. Chapter 5 focuses on Historical Significance (Unit F987) and brings together all of the skills and understandings acquired across the whole course of study.

How to use this book

Engagement with historical thinking needs to run throughout teaching and learning for OCR History B. *Historical Controversies and Historical Significance* has been written specifically to provide teachers and students with a taught course on the methodological understanding required for every topic and in every A2 exam unit.

Each unit in OCR History B is designed to be introduced through a consideration of the historical concepts. The modes of historical thinking should preface the start of every new topic and might also make valuable conclusions too. Teaching programmes might adopt a dynamic pattern of alternating between theory and topic content, the one buttressing, developing and reinforcing the other. This book will allow you to adopt either approach.

Methods of assessment

The Advanced GCE is made up of two mandatory units at AS and two further units at A2. There are three units at A2, of which candidates do two, either:

■ Unit F985 *Historical Controversies – British History* and Unit F987 *Historical Significance*

or

■ Unit F986 *Historical Controversies – Non-British History* and Unit F987 *Historical Significance*.

The Historical Controversies unit is assessed through an externally set, externally marked, task. Candidates answer two questions on their chosen period. The first question requires analysis of an extract or extracts from the work of one historian and asks what you can learn from the extract about the interpretation, approach or method of that historian. The second question asks how a particular approach has contributed to our understanding of the topic. Each question is worth a maximum of 30 marks and candidates have three hours to complete the task during a two-week period nominated by OCR.

Unit F987, the Personal Study, is concerned with the theory and assessment of historical significance. Candidates will be required to propose and produce a personal study of 3000 words and a research diary of 1000 words. Each study must be concerned with the significance of events, people or sites – either over time or across time or both. Unit F987 is internally assessed and externally moderated.

Notes for students

How to use this book

This book has been specifically written to support you through the OCR B GCE History course. *Historical Controversies and Historical Significance* will help you to understand the theory and concepts that underlie the topics you are studying. You should also refer back to this book during your revision. The Exam Café sections at the end of chapters 3 and 4 and on the CD-ROM will be particularly helpful as you prepare for the supervised task.

The book includes the following features:

Source **D** The importance of the Suez Canal to British trade

Egypt forms our highway to India and the East generally ... As regards the Suez Canal, England has a double interest; it has a predominant commercial interest, because 82% of the trade passing through the Canal is also to China where we have vast interests and 84% of the external trade of the still more enormous Empire. It is also one of the roads to our Colonial Empire in Australia and New Zealand.

- **Sources and passages**
  A wide variety of sources and extracts throughout the book will allow you to practise your historical skills.

- **For discussion**
  These have been designed to help you understand the specification content and develop your historical skills.

- **Think like an historian**
  You should be thinking like an historian throughout your history course. Questions are asked about the content to encourage you to think like this; sometimes you really should just think through these ideas!

FOR DISCUSSION

In a small group, discuss the difference between

THINK LIKE AN HISTORIAN

In your own words, summarise Pleuger's

- **Case studies**
  These encourage you to consider why historians create different interpretations of the same events and develop your own ideas and explanations.

Case study 2: The debate over Britain's seventeenth-cer crises, 1629–89

Introduction

Considerable historical debate surrounds the various crises in seventeenth-ce English – and British – history. This is particularly true for the causes and natur

- **Exam tips**
  These give you advice about exam preparation to help you achieve the best grade you can.

- **Quick facts and biographies**
  Additional background information in the margin will give you the wider context.

- **Definitions**
  Definitions of new words can be found in the margin close to where the word appears in the text to help put the word in context.

EXAM TIP

Before submitting your answer and moving on

QUICK FACTS

Tonnage and

Synchronic

Across time.

Which broad historical approach(es) could source D be used to

- **Activities**
  These will encourage you to consider different historical interpretations.

- **Stretch and challenge**
  Activities to extend your historical skills.

Stretch and challenge

Consider how concepts of race have changed over time.
How did this affect the ways in which empire was seen in the late nineteenth century?

- **Link up**
  To aid understanding, historical interpretations and approaches referred to in the case studies are cross referenced to explanations in chapters 1 and 2.

LINK UP

History and anthropology – see

- **Exam Café – print and electronic**
  In our unique Exam Café you'll find lots of ideas to help you prepare for the supervised task. You can **Relax** because there's handy revision advice from fellow students, **Refresh your memory** with summaries and checklists of the key ideas you need to revise and **Get that result!** through practising exam-style questions, accompanied by hints and tips on getting the very best grades.

ExamCafé
Relax, refresh, result!

Free CD-ROM

You'll also find a free CD-ROM in the back of the book. On the CD there's an electronic version of the Student Book, powered by LiveText. As well as the Student Book and LiveText tools, you will also find an interactive Exam Café. This contains a wealth of interactive supervised task preparation material: revision flashcards, checklists, exam-style questions with student answers and examiner feedback and much more!

Series Editor's introduction

Congratulations! You are studying the most exciting and useful of the six AS/A2 History specs. OCR's History B gets to grips with what History actually is. Famously, the author of *The Go-Between* said 'The past is a foreign country; they do things differently there'. Spec B will teach how to understand that other world: how to judge the surviving evidence; how to make sense of the past by putting that evidence together; how and why that evidence generates rival interpretations of the past; and how to measure the significance of people and their actions. Through spec B, you will see why History is alive with argument and debate, always being rethought and revised. Along the way, you will also learn to assess the motives of our ancestors and the consequences of their actions. That matters, for their decisions shaped our world; their tomorrows are our yesterdays.

Heinemann's series of books and CD-ROMs are tailored to spec B. Whichever topics you are studying, you have to learn how to think like a historian. This book will develop your thinking and understanding, and teach you the skills that you need for success. Ideas and issues are highlighted in text boxes. Case studies with sources, extracts and activities set you problems to consider. 'Think like an historian' questions encourage you to see the bigger picture. Exam tips work on your question skills. All will help you when you are starting to study a topic as well keeping you on course during the term – and don't forget them when revising for mocks and then the real thing. Don't overlook the Exam Café, which is not just for revision - its focused advice and help are always on hand. Tips, revision checklists and advice show you how to write better essays. Get the result! offers model answers with advice about how to improve your answers. The Exam Café CD-ROM has even more.

Historical controversies

Controversy and History go hand in hand. The role of historians is to ask questions about the past, interpret the sources and make judgements on the evidence deduced from those sources. During that process, different conclusions are often reached from the same body of evidence. It is those alternative perspectives that generate historical debate between historians. Sometimes scholars disagree violently. Other disagreements are more subtle. Either way, disagreement is normal and controversy is often the means by which our understanding improves. Controversy makes History a living subject. It is the life blood of History.

Interpretations are not themselves the past. They make claims about the past; History is constructed by historians from the evidence they use and the questions they ask. Interpretations are not evidence, so keep clear of trying to decide how reliable they are. Rather, ask *how* an historian has interpreted the evidence in response to the questions they asked. That will lead you to understand *how* differences in interpretation have been generated. In turn, that will let you make a reasoned evaluation of just *how* convincing an interpretation is. If you follow that path, you will be able to make reasoned judgements on the relative effectiveness of differing views – on *how* the evidence (factual material) is best understood and used in historical context.

Can the historian be 100 per cent neutral? To do so, they must divorce themselves from the outlook and interests of their own age. Is that possible? Interpretations reflect the circumstances in which they are made as well as they evidence they are drawing on and the intentions of those making them. Historians are part of their present and that gives them what Michael Stanford terms 'an angle of vision over the past' (*A Companion to the Study of History*, Blackwell, 1994, p.86). That is what makes their ideas interesting. All historical writing is, to some degree, the prisoner of its time. Historians impose their own hierarchies of significance on the events they select for consideration. Facts are refracted in our mind.

Totally neutral history is impossible. The more scholars try to achieve it, the less exciting their ideas become and the more dull their writing. Historians can, however, be objective and balanced, giving full weight to ideas with which they disagree. The objective historian grounds their interpretation on the very best set of evidence that they can gather. Objectivity is the goal.

Historical significance

When thinking about historical significance, historians measure the importance of an individual or event. Was one person/event more important than any other in making things happen (to develop or change or stay the same)? To ask that question is to want to know what was going on (change and development over time), not what was happening (lists of events). The long view allows historians to map the causal influences between events. Only if we see how each part relates to the whole can we work out what was significant. Historians need the big picture.

Assessment of the contemporary impact of a person/event gives one measure of significance. Assessment of the impact over time gives another. If compared and combined, we have a third. With each, the historian is setting a value to specific parts of the past. That value will be provisional and negotiable, but the value being estimated is historical significance. Think of two timelines, one set out by chronology and one set out by causal links. The first lists events. The second measures their impact. Only the second allows us to distinguish between the surface froth and the main tides.

A note on the cover

The power of good design. A British concept (left, by Alfred Leete, 1914) recycled in the USA (right, by James Montgommery Flagg, 1917) and the Soviet Union (centre, by Vasili Semenovich, 1927. The text says: 'You are not yet a member of the Cooperative. Sign up immediately!'

In the battle for the hearts and mind of civilian populations, the choice weapon of the twentieth century was the poster. All three here were recruiting posters: the fight against Germany in the case of the first two, the struggle to modernise agriculture and transform food production with the third. Commercial advertising seeks to influence public opinion and change behaviour. It offers a very specific interpretation. Is government advertising any different? At what point does government advertising become propaganda? Why did governments of the twentieth century try to mobilise public opinion far more than in previous centuries?

Martin D. W. Jones

Historical theories and interpretations

Introduction

'… agreement among historians is remarkably difficult to achieve, and historical events are open to a multiplicity of interpretations.' (A. Green and K. Troup (1999) *The Houses of History*, p. 6)

Units F985 and F986 concern the nature, origins and consequences of historical controversy. They build on the AS units, which covered historical explanation and the use of historical sources in constructing interpretations. The object of studying Historical Controversies is to develop your understanding of why historians, in the study of any major historical topic, to some extent disagree with each other and provide alternative interpretations. You will not be expected to judge the validity of one interpretation against another, but you will need to show that you understand how and why historians arrive at different conclusions, and that you appreciate the strengths and weaknesses of their approaches.

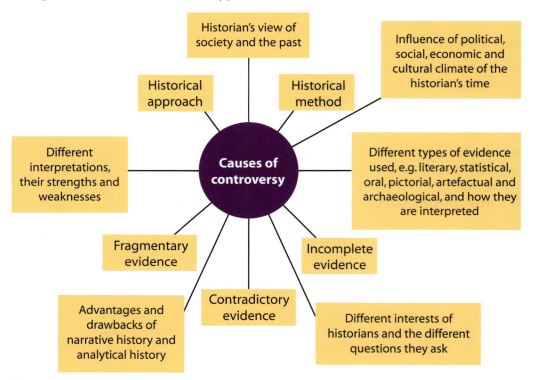

The causes of historical controversy

This chapter explores two key elements in the formation of historical interpretations:

■ The historian's view of human society and the past.
■ The role of theory.

Historical evidence

The problem every historian confronts, even when they are dealing with relatively recent historical events, is that the evidence they rely upon is likely to be:

■ fragmentary
■ incomplete
■ contradictory.

Everything surviving from the past that indicates some aspect of human activity is potential evidence for the historian. Thus the range of evidence is vast for *all* periods of history, and for all periods, it survives in fragmentary form. Some forms of evidence are more ephemeral than others. Some types of evidence were intentionally saved for posterity; others were thrown away as rubbish.

As a consequence of these factors, each historian's conclusions are influenced by:

- the selection of evidence used
- the interpretation of that evidence.

Furthermore, each generation of historians has access to a different range of evidence as some is lost and more is discovered.

THINK LIKE AN HISTORIAN

1. Consider one of the topics you studied for Unit F983 or Unit F984. What types of evidence are available to the historian for that topic? Make a list. Now consider how incomplete your understanding of that topic would be if only half of these were available to you. Write down your thoughts.

2. Think of an occasion when one source you consulted seemed to contradict another. How did this create a problem for you? How far, and in what ways, were you able to resolve this problem? Write down your observations.

3. What factors, other than available evidence, affect historians' interpretations?

Because of the fragmentary nature of evidence, historians need to be alert to the fact that they will never know everything about what happened in the past. This is what makes the subject so interesting: it may be concerned mostly with the lives of dead people but, as an academic discipline, it is full of life. Academic history is often described as 'organic' – it is continually developing, often in surprising ways. The academic historian, like the designer of a modern car, builds a new history which is based on a critical reflection of the old and the availability of new techniques and new materials.

Source (A)

Oak tree in winter at Lacock Abbey by pioneering photographer, Fox Talbot.

THINK LIKE AN HISTORIAN

Look at Source A.

1. Why is a tree such a suitable metaphor for both the past and the nature of the academic discipline of history?

2. Why do historical interpretations develop and change as time passes?

3. William Henry Fox Talbot, who produced this photograph, pioneered photography in England in the mid-nineteenth century. To what extent and why are photographs as historical evidence open to interpretation? Think of an example.

4. What effects, if any, do you think the advent of photography might have had upon the development of historical approaches and/or interpretations?

Historical questions and approaches

Historians approach sources with their own agenda. They all interrogate their sources, but the questions they ask are not always the same. These questions are shaped, in part, by what the historian is looking for. For example, an historian interested in gender issues is likely to ask different questions of the evidence for witch-hunting in early modern Europe from those of an historian interested in the history of religion.

Each historian's approach to the evidence is also determined, to a degree, by who they are: their ethnicity, sex, creed, and so on. For example, the feminist historian of such subjects as witch-hunting is, typically, female, and the **'subaltern' studies** of colonial and post-colonial India, typically, are those of Indian historians. Furthermore, the age in which the historians live is as likely as anything else to fashion their outlook and the questions they ask. The emergence of social history, discussed in the next chapter, for example, is very much associated with the emergence of the politics of socialism. In recent decades, many historians have adopted inter-disciplinary approaches and sometimes academics in other fields – sociologists, psychologists, anthropologists, etc. – have applied their subject-specific expertise to the construction of new histories.

As a result, modern history comprises a great range of approaches and perspectives, reflecting the diversity of the historians who write it. These include (among others):

- political history
- social history
- economic history
- cultural history
- gender history
- the history of class relations
- history 'from above'
- history 'from below'
- local history
- comparative history
- total history
- the history of mentalities.

Subaltern studies

This defines historical studies that focus on marginalised groups in a political structure, specifically those of the Indian sub-continent in the 'post-colonial' history that started to be written in the 1970s.

Categorisation and classification

Arguably, the one thing that binds historians together is their common objective in trying to make sense of the past. Since human life in the past was as complex as it is in the present, and the evidence is fragmented, this is a tall order. In trying to simplify things, historians have a habit of categorising the past by, for example, 'inventing' ages of history – the early medieval period, the later medieval, the early modern, the modern, and so on. As soon as they do so, they open themselves to criticism, as other historians reveal such things as periodisation to be nothing more than the artificial constructs of the historical community.

Here is an example. In the early nineteenth century, the curator of the National Museum of Denmark, Christian Thomsen, wanted to sort out his collection of ancient artefacts. Having some idea of the relative antiquity of each object, he was able to figure out that our earliest ancestors used tools made of stone; some of these, as well as new tools, subsequently came to be made bronze, and, eventually, a new range of tools appeared that was made of iron. Hence he devised a three age system for ordering the distant past:

- ■ Stone Age
- ■ Bronze Age
- ■ Iron Age.

Modern archaeologists are troubled by these definitions for the great epochs of prehistory. They complain that Thomsen seems to have neglected the fact that Stone Age people were at least as reliant on wood and other materials as they were on stone, and that wood, stone and many other materials were of huge importance in the ages after people started using metal. By naming his 'ages' after the material that survived, and ignoring that which did not, Thomsen had created a misleading impression of the past that survives to the present day. He seemed to have neglected the old adage: 'Absence of evidence is not evidence of absence'. Modern historians are as much engaged in reconstructing the past by trying to fill in the gaps in the evidence.

Even the most conservative of historians, suspicious of any 'simple' model of explanation for human behaviour and historical events, engages in the business of categorising and classifying the past. The periods into which the history of western Europe is divided are the convenient constructs of historians. In English history, for example, it is widely accepted for the sake of convenience that the medieval period ended on the battlefield at Bosworth in 1485. The Tudor dynasty ushered in a new historical epoch – 'the early modern period'. Every historian knows that this is a gross over-simplification of the very gradual historical processes that resulted in new modes of political, social and economic organisation, but it is convenient and helps historians give shape to a very complex past. These inventions classify historians themselves as they come to be tagged with labels such as 'medievalist', 'early modernist' and 'modernist' to reflect the spheres of their particular interest.

The habit of dividing the past into centuries poses a problem: while the passing of a century can influence history by creating a 'fin de siècle'/'turn of the century' mentality, many historical 'periods', such as reigns, straddle centuries. While, with the benefit of hindsight, the sixteenth century might 'look' different to the fifteenth, there were few, if any, fundamental differences in the world of the late 1490s and that of the early 1500s. A 'short' twentieth century has been identified by some historians which starts with the First World War (1914–18), a decisive historical turning point, and ends with another – the collapse of the Soviet Union in 1991. Arguably the historical 'era' in which we are now living began in the year 1991, not 2000.

In turn, people in the past are 'tagged' by historians. Diverse swathes of humanity are categorised with simple labels, for example 'peasants', 'proletarians', 'subalterns', 'radicals', 'reactionaries', 'protestants', and so on. It is tempting but erroneous for the historian to think of these as homogenous groups in which all individuals shared broadly the same outlook, values and life experience.

Much of the jargon used by historians would have been unfamiliar to the people they describe. For example, people living in the period between the demise of the classical civilisations and the Renaissance had no idea that they were living in the 'Middle Ages'. Furthermore, they would not have recognised their economic and political structures as the 'feudal system'. Detailed studies of feudalism defy a simple definition of the concept: historians of the impact of the Norman Conquest speak of a pre-1066 English version and a distinct Norman model. In both cases, it was still evolving; the term 'bastard feudalism' has been coined to describe the system in its fifteenth-century death throes. Historians spend a lot of time arguing over semantics, and it is right to question how far other historians have oversimplified or applied misnomers to the complexities of the past. Historians who are anxious not to exaggerate the phenomenon, or who prefer to find 'rational' explanations for seemingly irrational behaviour, reject the loaded term 'witchcraze' to describe witch-hunting in Europe in the early modern period as inappropriate since it implies that some kind of irrational mania was the root cause of the phenomenon.

The narrative approach

Traditionally, history writing was preoccupied with the writing of a narrative of the major political and cultural events in history and the life stories of the (mostly) men who precipitated these events. Description, as opposed to analysis, was its focus. A Level students soon learn that descriptive/narrative writing does not earn marks in examinations; however, as Ludmilla Jordanova has pointed out, description is of some value in the wider world of historical writing:

> 'Fine historical writing uses detail to further understanding. Perhaps "description" is misleading because it implies low-grade intellectual activity: simply recounting what is there. In fact, description is exceptionally telling because it selects pertinent details and thus, when well done, moves effortlessly into analysis. A brief yet vivid story or description can be an extremely effective distillation of a broader historical point. It makes what is past lively, immediate and interesting, and helps readers build up mental pictures.' (L. Jordanova (2006), *History in Practice*, p. 98)

In modern academic writing, analysis is the focus, whereas 'popular' histories continue to focus on 'the story'. If that story is a life history, probably the widest read form of history in the western world at the present time, it is likely to be told with a hefty amount of amateur psychoanalysis as the biographer explains the actions of their chosen personality.

In constructing narratives of the past, historians analyse evidence, choose what to discuss and what to leave out, and draw their own conclusions about how and why it developed as it did. Much modern academic writing focuses on historical themes rather than chronologies. Comparative studies provide opportunities for historians to contrast geographical areas, societies, and individuals which may or may not have been contemporaneous. Anthropologists have helped historians understand the past by observing human activities in modern societies.

Analysis invites interpretation. Interpretation leads to controversy and historical debate. The secure certainties of the past, at least in modern democracies, are no longer

THINK LIKE AN HISTORIAN

1. What distinguishes historical analysis from description?
2. What are the limitations of analysis without description?

accepted as they once were. Students, almost from the day they start studying History, are encouraged to question evidence and to recognise the possibility of alternative interpretations.

Whig history

Certain early British historians, taking an essentially narrative approach in their writing have come to be known as 'Whig' historians. The term 'Whig history' is often used to denote a triumphalist view of the past, one firmly wedded to the notion of progress. The term 'Whig' referred to the staunchly Protestant 'whiggamores' of late seventeenth-century Scotland and England who paved the way for the **Glorious Revolution** of 1688 and championed the values of political and civil liberty. No longer used as a term of contemporary political reference, unlike its counterpart 'Tory', it now refers to outmoded optimistic views of the past that celebrate the forming of the institutions of modern Britain. Consequently, the Whig historian 'adopted a nationalistic self-confidence that combined a patriotic sense of national qualities and uniqueness with an often xenophobic attitude towards foreigners, especially Catholics' (J. Black (1995) 'Whig history and lost causes', in *History Review*, December, p. 32).

Whig historians traced the evolution of these institutions through a series of constitutional struggles and triumphs that extended at least as far as the **Magna Carta** in the reign of King John. In so doing, their history was influenced by Darwin's theory of evolution. For Whig historians like Macaulay, Britain's political crises of the seventeenth century were part and parcel of the heroic struggle for political and religious liberty, rather than Hugh Trevor-Roper's subsequent cynical view of it as a desperate attempt by the old rural elite to restore their former status.

Historical concepts and theories

Since historical concepts and theories are so central to modern studies of history, it is worth considering the value of the theoretical approach. This is what historians Jeremy Black and Donald MacRaild have said on the matter:

> 'Concepts help us to order and clarify. They help historians to distinguish between essential and particular features of history. Concepts can also simplify historical problems, or at least our view of them. There are, of course, pitfalls. History is not easy, and there is rarely one answer to a problem (as the propensity of historians to "debates" suggests). Nor are concepts – created in the modern world and not used by the actors themselves – necessarily responsive to nuance. Historians invariably do simplify … selection, ordering and choice are all in the historian's vocabulary; but definitions imply simplification. A better term is "clarifying". Theory need not be jargon, and it can be enlightening. Historians should be open-minded about new ideas, for they may improve our insights into the past. To test ideas in the light of theoretical developments is to show humility and insight: this is the sign of a good historian.' (J. Black and D. MacRaild (2000) *Studying History*, p. 168)

History without theory is 'empirical' – it relies entirely upon the objective 'truth' some consider inherent in every piece of historical evidence. The problem with the strictly empirical approach is that as soon as the historian starts up a dialogue with the past through the questioning of the evidence, their personality comes to shape the history that is subsequently written. If subjectivity cannot be taken out of history, a compelling argument to which many subscribe, then the historian might as well accept this and begin to interpret the evidence on their own terms. Historians, like other people, are defined to a considerable extent by their points of view. In history, these are their theories. Arguably, all historians theorise, but some do it with more conviction than

others. Consequently, it stands to reason that 'Historians need to be able not just to recognise and name specific theoretical perspectives, but to have some idea of the properties of theories in general' (Jordanova (2006) , p. 57).

Empirical approaches to history are based on the assumption that theories/hypotheses/ interpretations should be assessed according to how far they 'stand up' to the evidence. Consequently, 'empiricists' rely on the principle that reliable evidence about the past exists. In the twentieth century, the discipline became preoccupied with the skills deployed by the historian in the finding and reading of the evidence. It was widely accepted that only through the most careful analysis of a source would the historian avoid the numerous pitfalls that could lead to misinterpretation.

What is History?

'The study of history, then amounts to a search for the truth.' (G. R. Elton (1969) *The Practice of History*, p. 70)

Not all historians believe an objective historical 'truth' can be attained. It has been argued that, ultimately, history is interpretation. It is an idea of what the past may have been like and, probably, an explanation for why it was as it was. History is not the past but a collection of views of the past. The point has been made succinctly by the historian Keith Jenkins:

> 'Let us say you have been studying part of England's past – the sixteenth century – at A level. Let us imagine that you have used one major text-book: Elton's *England under the Tudors*. In class you have discussed aspects of the sixteenth century, you have class notes, but for your essays and the bulk of your revision you have used Elton. When the exam came along you wrote in the shadow of Elton. And when you passed, you gained an A level in English history, a qualification for considering aspects of "the past". But really it would be more accurate to say you have an A level in Geoffrey Elton: for what, actually, at this stage, is your "reading" of the English past if not basically his reading of it?' (K. Jenkins (1991) *Rethinking History*, p. 7)

History, therefore, is a view of the past seen through subsequent layers of interpretation, building up across generations of historians like the layers of sediment obscuring the ruins of an ancient culture. As historians look to the past, they encounter, analyse and revise the interpretations of their predecessors.

FOR DISCUSSION

In a small group, consider the following:

Is the history written long after the events themselves any more or less reliable than that written soon after?

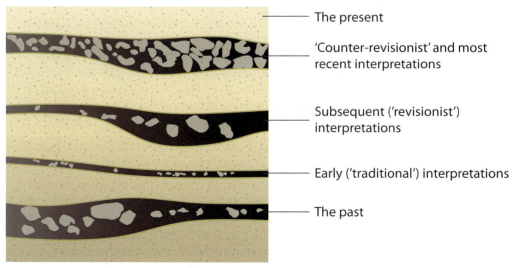

How layers of historical interpretation are built up

Consequently, it can be argued that history *is* **historiography** since it is all to do with the evaluation of previous interpretations in the fashioning of new ones or, in the case of a '**counter-revisionist**' interpretation, the restoration of older arguments. As the historian E. H. Carr in *What is History?* stated: 'The historian is part of history. The point in the procession at which he finds himself determines his angle of vision over the past' (Carr (1964), p. 36). Perversely, however, hindsight provides historians with the argument that, despite this, they 'in a way know more about the past than the people who lived it' (Jenkins (1991), p. 13).

> ### THINK LIKE AN HISTORIAN
>
> Why can it be claimed that historians 'know more about the past than the people who lived it'?

Such **postmodernist** arguments are fine to a point, but more traditional-minded historians are deeply critical of views that suggest that history is simply subjective story-telling based on incomplete and problematic evidence. Some history, in the view of Richard Evans, can/should only be read one way:

> 'The gas chambers were not a piece of rhetoric. Auschwitz was indeed inherently a tragedy and cannot be seen as either a comedy or a farce.' (Richard Evans (1997), *In Defence of History,* quoted in Black and MacRaild (2000), p. 166)

Historical interpretations

Postmodernism is the term that has been applied over the past 50 years to ways in which the 'modern' ideas of the twentieth century in academic disciplines, including philosophy, literature and history, have been challenged. A central theme in 'postmodern' history is the theory that the pursuit of an objective truth about the past is misguided. Just as 'postmodern' literary critics have argued that literary criticism reveals more about the critic/reader than the author, 'postmodern' history theorists argue that historians should focus on the processes by which written history is formed. Hence it encourages a laudably critical, but gloomily sceptical, reading of historical sources.

Chance in history

> 'Nothing is inevitable until it happens.' (A. J. P. Taylor in *The Daily Telegraph*, 7 January 1980)

According to John Tosh, 'Historians spend most of their time explaining change – or its absence' (J. Tosh (1984) *The Pursuit of History*, p. 129). In this respect, medieval monkish chroniclers had it easy: for them all things were ordained by God and both the predictable and unpredictable events that unfurled were all the consequence of divine providence. If there was any human agency involved in why things happened, it was to do with divine punishment for human sinfulness. Human history was placed in the context of an inexorable march towards the end of the world and the Last Judgement.

When God is taken out of the picture, historians have a stark choice: they can either accept that everything is the product of chance and random circumstances, or they can devise their own **determinist theories** and explanations that may or may not be part of the Creator's great plan. As this chapter will demonstrate, determinist explanations certainly exist, but it is appropriate to start by pointing out that plenty of historians reject such explanations entirely. This is explained by John Tosh:

Historiography

The study of historians and their writing about the past. It is the history of history writing and the factors determining historical accounts and interpretations.

Counter-revisionist

An argument that challenges the claims of history which 'revises' the traditional view. There is no 'school' of counter-revisionist historians and the term needs to be used with caution.

Postmodernism

The term is sometimes used to describe new ways of viewing the past that have evolved since the late twentieth century.

Determinist theories

Theories based on the assumption that events are determined by previous circumstances.

BIOGRAPHY

A. J. P. Taylor, English historian (1906–90), was well known for his controversial comments on the major events of the twentieth century, including the origins of the Second World War. Sometimes his interpretations seemed to other historians to have been produced merely for the sake of provoking an argument. He became well known later in his career through his hugely popular televised lectures.

THINK LIKE AN HISTORIAN

Is History a 'social science'? Explain your answer.

Social Darwinism

Building on the theory of Charles Darwin (1809–92) that evolution is determined by the success of the 'fittest' in the evolutionary struggle, Social Darwinism applies the idea to the development of human societies. The theory was used as a justification for the claims of supremacy of one ethnic group over another in the first half of the twentieth century in the right-wing dictatorships of western Europe.

'These grounds for rejecting theories of history are closely related to another argument which has often been given heavy emphasis: that theory denies not only the "uniqueness" of events but also the dignity of the individual and the power of human agency. Traditional narrative shorn of any explanatory framework gives maximum scope to the play of personality, whereas a concern with recurrent or typical aspects of social structure and social change elevates abstraction at the expense of real living individuals. Worst of all from this viewpoint are theories … whose insidious effect is to confer an inevitability on the historical process which individuals are powerless to change, now or in the future; all theories of history, the argument goes, have determinist elements, and determinism is a denial of human freedom. The polar opposite of determinism is the rejection of any meaning in history beyond the play of the contingent and the unforeseen – a view held by many historians in the mainstream of the discipline. **A. J. P. Taylor** delights in informing his readers that the only lesson taught by the study of the past is the incoherence and unpredictability of human affairs: history is a chapter of accidents and blunders.' (Tosh (1984), p. 132)

These 'accidents and blunders' make for a situation which, some would argue, is far too complex and unique to be explained away by the convenient theories of social scientists. In the view of one modern historian, it is in the historian's very nature to question theoretical models in any explanation of past events:

'[the] critical attitude to minutiae has become in the end the powerful agent of selection. It now attracts to history persons of a cautious and painstaking disposition, not necessarily endowed with any aptitude for theoretical synthesis' (M. M. Postan, quoted in Tosh (1984), p. 133).

In any case, evidence in support of any theory is likely to be found with a little imagination and if the historian looks hard enough. After all, as Aileen Kraditor has pointed out in the case of American historical studies, the range of source material is vast and often contradictory:

'If one historian asks, "Do the sources provide evidence of militant struggles among workers and slaves?" the sources will reply, "Certainly". And if another asks, "Do the sources provide widespread acquiescence in the established order among the American population throughout the past two centuries?" the sources will reply, "Of course".' (Quoted in Tosh (1984), p. 130)

For some, theoretical models of explanation are not just wrong, they are also dangerous. They prepare the ground for and justify experiments in social engineering. This, after all, was the experience of Nazi-occupied Europe which was slave to the creed of '**Social Darwinism**'.

Divine explanation aside, that chance to some degree plays a role in history is undeniable. Natural disasters such as volcanoes, floods and epidemics, have been powerful factors in shaping the course of history. The chance outcomes of battles in which, for example, a stray arrow kills a leader, have had serious consequences. Seven types of chance in history have been identified by Gilbert Pleuger in *History Review*:

'The place of chance in history can be differentiated. Firstly, there is that chance which is the sudden activity of an aspect of nature. It can be weather (serious drought, unusual precipitation and flood), or geomorphological disaster (earthquake or volcano), or disease. The Black Death, 1349, and the 1590s plague in Spain are examples of the latter. Secondly, war and battle condenses and accelerates relationships and magnifies the consequences of the minor and the unpredictable act, because in a battle or war there is less opportunity for action to counter the unexpected and unpredictable. The death of Gustavus Adolphus while in dense fog at the battle of Lützen, 1632, is a well known example. Thirdly, if historians allow a place to the potency of individual action they need also to allow that a man may act unpredictably, irrationally or in a way inappropriate to his needs and wishes, because of misjudgement or confusion. Napoleon III's paralysis of decision in January 1871 during the Franco-Prussian war may be seen as an illustration. Fourthly, situations of even, pivotal, balance within and between states and societies or institutions may magnify beyond normal proportions the consequences of singular events and individual acts. The attempt of Charles I to arrest the Five Members, 1642, may be seen in this way as also the actions of Boris Yeltsin, symbolized by the picture of him on a tank, during the days of the attempted coup in August [1991]. Similarly, and fifthly, when social and institutional inertia is reduced and society, its government and economy, have less stability the actions of individuals have greater decisiveness. This is a tenable, if unfashionable, view of German history between 1928 and 1932. Sixthly, if we accept any kind of stratification of type of event and relationship a change at one level may, in the unusual circumstance, influence not only "its" level but be important in other levels. It can now be seen, for example, that the minor administrative decision to place a maximum price for Castilian grain in 1539 had consequences far beyond the agrarian and significantly influenced Spain at the economic, demographic, social and military levels. Seventhly and lastly, the form of chance that receives more explicit recognition in historical accounts, is the accident. The deaths of William III in 1702 and Sir Robert Peel in 1850, after riding accidents, are examples.' (G. Pleuger (1992) 'Chance in history', *History Review*, March, pp. 22–3)

Jeremy Black, who has written extensively on the theory and practice of History, has highlighted the importance of chance in history by commenting on the activities of war-gamers:

> 'Military history is the most obvious field in which it is dangerous to adopt the perspective of hindsight. War-gamers devote their time to an entirely reasonable pastime, asking whether battles, campaigns and conflicts could have had different results. Could the Jacobites have won, the British have defeated the American Revolutionaries or the Confederates triumphed in the American Civil War? Recent work has thrown doubt on any determinist technological approach to the history of warfare, and the role of chance and contingent factors of terrain, leadership quality, morale, the availability of reserves and the unpredictable spark that ignites a powder magazine, appear crucial when explaining particular engagements. War is not always won by the big battalions and the determinist economic account that would explain success in international relations in terms of the economic strength of particular states ... is open to serious question.' (Black (1995), p. 33)

Since the outcome of campaigns has had such a huge impact in history, these are very important considerations. The war-gamer perhaps is presented with something approaching a real opportunity to set up scientific experiments for testing claims of inevitability in history. However, the complexities of a military struggle as vast as, say, the English Civil War, probably make this a forlorn hope.

Intentionalist interpretations: case study

In evaluating the British policy of appeasement in the 1930s, historians need to consider the situation facing the prime minister Chamberlain and his government. How far was Hitler in control of German foreign policy? Did he have a pre-planned foreign policy with clear aims? A. J. P. Taylor argued that Hitler was an opportunist who capitalised on Chamberlain's blunders, whereas Hugh Trevor-Roper believed he had a

---

THINK LIKE AN HISTORIAN

In your own words, summarise Pleuger's seven types of chance in history. Suggest additional historical examples to illustrate these.

THINK LIKE AN HISTORIAN

Make two lists of historical events: one mainly caused by intent, one mainly caused by chance. Show your list to another member of your group. Do they agree with your decisions? If not, why not?

master-plan that could be traced back to the pages of his 1920s autobiography *Mein Kampf* ('My Struggle'), his 'blueprint' for future war. Trevor-Roper's argument that the Second World War was the realisation of this master-plan can be defined as an intentionalist interpretation in which history is driven by human agency: in this case, Hitler.

Structural interpretations

The discipline of sociology has had a great impact upon the work of historians. Sociologists have studied the social structures that help determine the behaviour of both the 'socialised' and the 'deviant'. Structuralist historians have fused the sociologists' interest in structures with the new interest of twentieth-century historians in social and economic history. The culture of the societies they investigate is regarded as having a 'super-structure' of ideas, such as religious and folkloric beliefs, and institutions, such as political and legal structures, which are determined by the base structure. For Marxist historians, this is the economic system upon which society is based (see Marxist interpretations below).

Historical determinism

Social historians and sociologists interested in the past have looked for underlying historical trends in their analyses. These are the dynamic forces – the historical processes such as the struggle between classes – that have shaped history.

Black and MacRaild have explained how Keith Thomas provided a determinist interpretation for such things as witchcraft beliefs and witch hunts:

> 'Keith Thomas's major study of belief, *Religion and the Decline of Magic* (1971), was heavily influenced by the [**Annalist**] **School** … Thomas argued: 'One of the central features was a preoccupation with the explanation and relief of human misfortune'. In this respect, by painting an image of a people locked in fear of their world, [writers like Thomas] shared Braudel's social determinism – the idea that the world was shaped by forces extraneous to humankind.' (Black and MacRaild (2000), p. 79)

The identification of such profound forces in the present and the past has led sociologists, political philosophers and historians into the forming of 'scientific' theories to explain historical change. They have aimed 'to uncover the dynamic of history – that which gives it motion' (Black and MacRaild (2000), p. 134).

Profound causes – the 'Frontier thesis'

The French Annalist historians, discussed in the next chapter, advocated a 'total' history that considered the influence of profound causes as well as specific events in the formulation of interpretations regarding why things happened as they did in the past. In his investigation of the emergence of the institutions of the USA, **Frederick Jackson Turner** declared in 1893: 'Behind institutions, behind constitutional forms and modifications, lie the vital forces that call these organs into life and shape them to meet changing conditions' (quoted in Marwick (1970), *The Nature of History*, p. 70). In Turner's interpretation, these 'vital forces' were unique and conditioned by the drive to extend the frontier of white settlement:

> 'The peculiarity of American institutions is the fact that they have been compelled to adapt themselves to the changes of an expanding people – to the changes involved in crossing a continent, in winning a wilderness, and in developing at each area of this progress out of the primitive economic and political conditions of the frontier into the complexity of city life.' (Quoted in Marwick (1970), p. 70)

Although Turner would be criticised for neglecting the European roots of American civilisation and for failing to undertake a comparative study of other 'frontier' histories, his perception of the profundities of historical causation were hugely influential.

Metanarratives

The 'Frontier thesis' is an excellent example of what might be described in some interpretations as a 'metanarrative', that is, a major text (e.g. the Bible, the Communist Manifesto), a scientific principle (e.g. Darwinism/Social Darwinism) or myth (e.g. Aryan supremacy, witchcraft) used by a society to help explain its past and present, and to help unite that society in a common purpose.

Marxist interpretations

> 'Some would argue that … the very heart of human activity is dominated by an oscillation between two opposites, the *idea* and the *economic prerogative*.' (Marwick (1970), p. 73)

The most influential determinist explanation concerning the historical process is that of the political philosopher, Karl Marx. In the mid-nineteenth century, Marx, together with Friedrich Engels, developed a theory which was concerned with the conflict between opposing forces. This was to become the foundation of the principle that in history the force that leads to change is the struggle between social classes. Since this struggle was to do with the nature of the provision of human material needs (food, shelter, clothing), Marx concluded that, though other things such as scientific discoveries, are important, the driving force in history is economics (**economic determinism**). Until society developed a system that was satisfactory for all (**communism**), this struggle would continue. Only when all inequality was destroyed, and hence society became classless, would this struggle cease. Since Marxist history is to do with change, the establishment of the classless, communist society could be described as the end of history.

Marxist history is essentially a **positivist approach** since it works on the principle that the historical dynamic inevitably drives society towards the communist resolution of the class struggle. Marx and Engels identified three stages through which all human society must pass before it developed the economic structure – communism – that ended class conflict.

Stage 1: the Ancient – the slave-driven economies of classical Greece and Rome.

Stage 2: the Feudal – the lord and serf system of obligations associated with the medieval period.

Stage 3: the Bourgeois – the capitalist system in which cash payments, rather than obligations, became the 'nexus' (link) in the relationship between the classes (i.e. '**bourgeois**' entrepreneurs and '**proletarian**' workers).

The final epoch, communism, would emerge from the overthrowing of the capitalist system and the destruction of the concept of class by giving the producers (the workers) communal ownership of everything they produced. Until this stage, the mode of production was bound to lead to tension and conflict: slaves would rebel against slave-owners, serfs against lords, workers against employers. As the highly stratified world of medieval Europe was reduced to two powerful classes – the 'bourgeoisie' and the 'proletariat' – the stage was set for a final violent showdown: the revolution(s) that would eliminate the bourgeoisie and its capitalist system for good.

Consequently, for Marxist historians, economics largely determines the nature of society, including its cultural as well as political aspects, at every point in the past. In

---

Economic determinism

The theory that the driving force, the 'dynamic', of history is economic structure.

Communism

Associated with the ideas of Karl Marx and earlier nineteenth century philosophers and political theorists, communism defines an economic system based upon complete social and economic equality, and a political system that is classless and stateless. The goal of communism became associated in the late nineteenth and twentieth centuries with the more extreme exponents of socialist politics.

Positivist approach

An approach that presumes natural/scientific 'laws' determine the course of history.

Bourgeois

Literally 'of the middle classes'; the term used by Karl Marx to define the business class/middle class that he stated 'owned' the labour of the working class.

Proletarian

Term favoured by Karl Marx to define the waged working class, whose labour he maintained was controlled/owned by the 'bourgeoisie'.

Marx's opinion, everything was influenced by the economic structure of the epoch in which people live:

> 'The mode of production of material life conditions the process of social, political and intellectual life. It is not the consciousness of men that determines their existence but their social existence that determines their consciousness.' (Karl Marx, from the preface to *Contribution to the Critique of Political Economy* (1859))

Thus Marx challenged the conventional view that the ideas of men and women shaped their destinies. Consequently, historians of beliefs that resulted in such episodes as the witch hunts of early modern Europe and the Holocaust of the twentieth century argue over the extent to which ideas determined events or whether they were the product, like every other part of the social 'super-structure', of the economic base upon which it was founded.

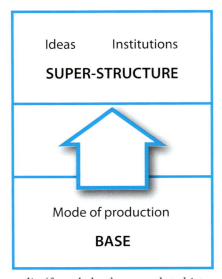

Marxist version of the structuralist 'from below' approach to history

Marxist analyses, focusing on class struggle, have been directed at most of the major themes of modern historical studies including the nature of Norman feudalism, the English Civil War/revolution and other seventeenth-century crises, and the causes of nineteenth-century imperialism.

Having identified what he believed to be the natural law of history, Marx was able to claim that future developments could be predicted. These lofty philosophical claims, of course, are anathema to historians who believe that history is the product of chance and coincidence. For postmodernists, the difficulty, even impossibility, of arriving at an objective 'truth' in the historical interpretation of evidence, prevents historians from finding universal laws equivalent to the natural laws of science.

Ludmilla Jordanova explains why Marxist interpretations have a much lower profile now than they did in the recent past:

> 'Until about 20 years ago, most people would have come up with Marxism if asked to name a theory important to the practice of history. Now there appear to be few attempts to develop Marxian historiography further. We could interpret this shift in a number of ways. It could indicate disenchantment with the world view that Marxism represented. It could suggest that its key elements have already been incorporated where they are useful. Perhaps just fragments of Marxism remain alive. It is possible that, because of cultural shifts, historians have lost interest in the leading themes of Marxism, such as class struggle and the nature of production, because they ceased to be apt for the world we now inhabit. Intellectual fashions do

THINK LIKE AN HISTORIAN

How has 'the world view' regarding Marxism changed in the last quarter century?

change, as a result of which theories fall out of favour, less because of explicit criticisms than because they are no longer vital and relevant.' (Jordanova (2006), p. 57)

Stretch and challenge

Ask your teacher for a copy of the article in the teacher's LiveText entitled 'Marxist history: the century of revolution, 1603–1714'.

1. What phrases and passages reveal Hill's Marxist perspective?

2. Try placing Hill's seventeenth-century 'English Revolution' within the framework of Marx's stages of history.

History and progress

Most modern historians are less convinced than many of their 'positivist' Whig predecessors regarding the optimistic view that history is essentially the story of human progress. This revision of old ideas has been summarised by Lawrence Stone:

'Today we are uneasily aware that for long periods of time, as long as a century or more, Europe has in fact stagnated or regressed. The first, longest, and most tragic of such intermissions lasted from about 1320 to 1480, and covered the whole of Europe with the exception of Italy. During this dismal period, governmental authority crumbled as local warlordism grew, tax yields declined, and the state became a prey of aristocratic factions. Worse still, a **Malthusian crisis**, followed by recurrent attacks of devastating bubonic plague, prolonged Anglo-French war, and erratic monetary manipulation combined drastically to reduce both the population and the production and trade of Europe. Population shrank even faster than production so that real income *per capita* rose and the poor were probably economically better off than ever before, or than they were to be again until the mid-nineteenth century. But the psychological impact of living in a contracting world, with a horribly low expectation of life, was very high indeed. As Huizinga showed many years ago, the fifteenth century was an age of melancholy and morbid introspection.' (L. Stone (1981), *The Past and the Present*, p. 133)

The subsequent Renaissance and Reformation, and the emergence of modern capitalism in place of medieval feudalism, could have heralded a lasting pattern of progress, but they did not. Instead, for Europe the seventeenth century is perceived as another age of stagnation or regression – an age of crises:

'In … Germany, there raged for thirty years a war as destructive of civilian lives and property as any of this [twentieth] century, and much of the area was left in ruins … Even England, which, thanks to the improvement in agricultural productivity and the extraordinary prosperity of its colonial trade after 1660, was only mildly affected by the Great Depression, saw its population stagnate, its trade endure a prolonged crisis of readjustment from 1620 to 1660, and its output of iron, lead and tin level off … the mid-seventeenth century saw a crisis in the growth of the nation state … the 1640s were the decade during which major upheavals occurred in England, Ireland, Scotland, France, Sweden, Catalonia, Portugal and Naples, there was a coup in Holland, and Germany endured the final, desperate, convulsions of the Thirty Years War.' (Stone (1981), p. 134)

In his consideration of the English Civil War, Britain's greatest crisis of the seventeenth century, Stone has shown how historians can arrive at radically different interpretations

---

Malthusian crisis

Thomas Malthus (1766–1834) is sometimes seen as the founder of the historical approach known as 'demography' (the study of population). The 'Malthusian crisis' marked the moment at which population growth outstripped the supply of food. Nature, he believed, left to its own devices, 'checked' such a crisis by such means as epidemic disease – unfortunate, but ultimately necessary, facts of life.

THINK LIKE AN HISTORIAN

Use a suitable resource to construct a timeline of major events in a part of Europe during the fifteenth century. How far does the evidence substantiate Stone's claim?

FOR DISCUSSION

In a small group, consider the following:

What arguments can be made for and against the proposition that 'History is progress'?

regarding whether a major historical event should be perceived as a human triumph or a disaster, an example of progress or regression.

'What happened in England in the middle of the seventeenth century? Was it a "great rebellion" as Clarendon believed, the last and most violent of the many rebellions against particularly unprepossessing or unpopular kings, that had been staged by dissident members of the landed classes century after century throughout the Middle Ages? Was it merely an internal war caused by a temporary political breakdown due to particular political circumstances? Was it the Puritan revolution of S. R. Gardiner, to whom the driving force behind the whole episode was a conflict of religious institutions and ideologies? Was it the first great clash of liberty against royal tyranny, as seen by Macaulay, the first blow of ... **Whiggery**, a blow which put England on the first bourgeois revolution, in which the economically progressive and dynamic elements in society struggled to emerge from their feudal swaddling clothes? This is how Engels saw it, and how many historians of the 1930s, including R. H. Tawney and C. Hill, tended to regard it. Was it the first revolution of modernization, which is the Marxist interpretation in a new guise, now perceived as a struggle of entrepreneurial forces to remould the institutions of government to meet the needs of a more efficient, more rationalistic, and more economically advanced society? Or was it a revolution of despair, engineered by the decaying and backward-looking elements in rural society, the mere gentry of H. R. Trevor-Roper, men who hoped to recreate the decentralised, inward-looking, socially stable and economically stagnant society of their hopeless, anachronistic dreams?' (Stone, p. 182)

Whiggery

'History that is written either from the point of view of the winners or from an unthinking commitment to progress. The term implies criticism of such an approach.'
(Jordanova (2006), p. 230)

THINK LIKE AN HISTORIAN

Copy out the table below and, in your own words, summarise the interpretations of the historians mentioned by Stone.

Historian	Interpretation
Edward Hyde, 1st Earl of Clarendon (1609–74), author of *History of the Rebellion and Civil Wars in England*	
S. R. Gardiner (1829–1902), historian of the English Civil War and the Protectorate	
Thomas Babington Macaulay, 1st Baron Macaulay (1800–59), politician and author of *The History of England from the Accession of James II*	
Friedrich Engels (1820–95), co-author with Karl Marx of *The Communist Manifesto* (1848)	
R. H. Tawney (1880–1962), co-founder of the Economic History Society in 1926	
Christopher Hill (1912–2003), Marxist historian of England's seventeenth-century revolution	
Hugh Trevor-Roper (1914–2003), historian of early modern Britain and Nazi Germany	

'From above' and 'from below' interpretations

Historians argue about the influence of the elite and the masses on events. This is especially true of social history, such as that of witchcraft beliefs in the early modern period, but also underpins many of the debates surrounding 'political' events such as revolutions. Arthur Marwick, for example, has commented on 'from below' interpretations of the British government's policy of appeasement in the late 1930s:

> 'Much was once made of "pacifist" British public opinion which is supposed to have deterred Britain's Conservative Government from taking the action it really believed to be desirable: the labours of D. C. Watt and some early work of my own have, I hope, done something to dispel this nonsense – "public opinion" and government formed a confused continuum in which pacifism was one element, but never a dominant one.' (Marwick (1970), p. 275)

It is often difficult to divorce the attitude of the elite from that of the masses. For example, the enthusiasm with which Neville Chamberlain was greeted in 1938 on his return from securing the Munich agreement with Hitler was share by both the king, George VI, and his people. Similarly, the fundamental beliefs in magic, witchcraft, and the devil, upon which witch-hunting in early modern Europe relied, were universal concepts that were not 'class-bound', although the support for such beliefs 'from above' may well have been a crucial element in the persecution of ordinary people by their neighbours (i.e. 'from below').

Historians, however, are generally alert to the likelihood that the mentality of one socio-political group of people in the past was likely to be significantly different from that of another. Indeed, the conflict between different classes could be a significant force in the creation of *opposing* mentalities. This, according to Brian Levack, appears to have been the case in the history of the decline of witch-hunting:

> 'The persistence of superstitious beliefs among the peasantry may have actually contributed, in a somewhat ironic way, to the triumph of scepticism among the elite. One of the tactics that sceptics like Nicholas de Malebranche, Laurent Bordelon and Cyrano de Bergerac used to win support for their views was to ridicule the beliefs of the silly rustic shepherds and other peasants who continued to claim that witches were active in their communities. The same tactics of ridicule and satire, it should be noted, were later used by William Hogarth and Francisco Goya in the paintings and engravings they made on the theme of witchcraft and superstition. The effect of this ridicule was to encourage those who occupied the upper strata of society, even those who were not well-educated, to give at least lip-service to the new scepticism, so as to confirm their superiority over the lower classes. Scepticism, in other words, became fashionable. During the late seventeenth and early eighteenth centuries the barriers that separated the aristocracy and the wealthy from those who occupied the lower strata of society began to widen throughout Europe. In order to put as much distance as possible between themselves and the common people, the landowners and members of the professions, especially those who were upwardly mobile, did all they could to prove that they shared nothing with their inferiors. Knowledge of the latest scientific discoveries may have been one way to establish one's social and intellectual credentials, but scepticism regarding witchcraft, since it involved the expression of open contempt for the lower orders, was far more effective. The decline of witch beliefs among the wealthy and educated elite may have had as much to do with social snobbery as with the development of new scientific and philosophical ideas.' (B. Levack (3rd edn, 2006) *The Witch-Hunt in Early Modern Europe*, p. 269)

THINK LIKE AN HISTORIAN

1. For what reasons, according to Levack, did scepticism regarding witchcraft beliefs, increase in the late seventeenth and early eighteenth centuries?

2. Is the extract from Levack a 'from above' or 'from below' explanation for the decline of witch-hunting? Explain your answer.

The 'subaltern' studies of the Indian experience of British colonialism are also, by definition, history 'from below'.

'From above' interpretations favour a narrative approach, particularly that of the biography of the 'great men' and women of history. 'From below' interpretations are more likely to highlight the place of structures, such as those of class or mentality, in the shaping of past events. Black and MacRaild have provided an interesting account of the dilemma faced by a structuralist historian who set out to write a biography:

> 'When Ian Kershaw was first approached to write a biography of Hitler, he was dubious about the utility of such an exercise, because, as a structuralist historian, he was more interested in wider aspects of the Third Reich and German history than in the Führer himself. As Kershaw approached the task, he found himself battling to understand "the man who was the indispensable fulcrum and inspiration of what took place, Hitler himself", while trying simultaneously to "downplay rather than to exaggerate the part played by the individual, however powerful, in complex historical processes" (*Hitler: 1889–1936: Hubris,* vol. I (1998)). This juxtaposition of seemingly contradictory forces illustrates well the tension inherent in writing historical biography.' (Black and MacRaild (2000), p. 104)

Stretch and challenge

Ask your teacher for a copy of the article in the teacher's LiveText entitled 'History from below: growing up in the Third Reich'. This provides a fascinating account of the era from the perspective of a former young 'Nazi'. When you have finished reading it, write a brief evaluation of history 'from below'.

Psychoanalytical interpretations

Biographical approaches to history invite psychoanalytical explanations. The histories that identify 'great men' as the movers and shakers in the shaping of the past are bound to consider the psychological make-up of the leading protagonists. Ludmilla Jordanova has provided a contemporary perspective on the state of play regarding acceptance in historical circles of this approach:

> 'Although still regarded with suspicion in some quarters, it has become an accepted part of the historian's theoretical armoury, especially in the United States, where many large history departments include a psychohistorian on the staff, and where special training courses are available to scholars who want to use psychoanalysis in their research but have no wish to develop clinical skills. Yet most people, and scholars are no exception, think psychoanalytically without being particularly aware of doing so. Many of the explanations we give of behaviour in everyday life owe much to what are now commonplace assumptions about how the unconscious works. Since a significant proportion of historical explanation rests on such assumptions, psychoanalysis has found its way into historical practice. However, many historians still have little direct knowledge of psychoanalytical thinking or of the significant differences between its principal traditions: Freudian, Jungian, Kleinian and Lancanian. There have been attacks on psychoanalysis in history, as there have been on psychoanalysis in general.' (Jordanova (2006), p. 57)

THINK LIKE AN HISTORIAN

To what extent, and why, is historical interpretation subject to changing intellectual fashions?

For the study of such issues as the Holocaust and early modern witch-hunting, psycho-historians have engaged in investigations into collective psychology to understand why such phenomena could, at best, be greeted with widespread indifference and, at worst, with enthusiasm. Consequently, psycho-history can be as much to do with 'from below' interpretations as it is with those 'from above'.

Feminist history

'Research during the last 15 years or so has resulted in a major new discovery. It now appears that, contrary to all assumptions, *there were women in English history.*' (K. Charlesworth and M. Cameron (1986) *All That … The Other Half of History*, Pandora, quoted in K. Sayer (1994) 'Feminism and History', in *Modern History Review*, November, p. 7)

Karen Sayer has explained why, in the words of Virginia Woolf, 'women have no history':

'Until relatively recently, despite notable exceptions, history was written by and for men, especially white academic men. This was, and still is, the structural problem, built into the production of knowledge, that Virginia Woolf attacked. Those who write history have decided what is significant, so that women have been excluded and hidden … The prevalent view was that historians should only be concerned with change and with major political and economic movements. As women did not play a decisive role in such processes, because women were supposed to be wives and mothers who did not take part in national decision-making, industry etc., they were not believed to be a legitimate subject of history.' (Sayer (1994), p. 5)

Since the 1960s, great strides have been taken in writing the story of groups hitherto 'hidden from history'. Not surprisingly, the bulk of the work on women's history has been done by women historians, typically those of a 'feminist' persuasion. A pioneering social historian, Joan Thirsk, on this point, has commented that:

'It is not usual to distinguish the work of women historians from those of men, though it is always instructive to do so. Their different lives make for different viewpoints and yield different insights; hence, in practice, they frequently choose distinctive themes for investigation, have their own styles in research and presentation, and rank their objectives and priorities differently. In the fields of local and family history especially, their insights are likely to be original and influential, since much of women's energy is devoted to creating and maintaining families and sustaining communities. But other signs of their individuality are likely to stem from their stronger sympathy for animate creatures than for inanimate things, and their keen observation of social relationships.' (Quoted in D. Hey (1996) *The Oxford Companion to Local and Family History*, p. 498)

Sayer has identified three stages in the development of writing about the history of women:

Stage 1: pre-1960s writings about the lives of *exceptional women*, i.e. women who in their lifetimes made an impact in a 'man's world' but who had since been largely forgotten. For example, the playwright, poet and novelist Aphra Behn (1640–89), and the late seventeenth-century English traveller and writer Celia Fiennes.

Stage 2: *women's contribution* history – the re-exploration of major themes involving a search for the women who contributed to historical developments previously associated with men. For example, the work of Dorothy Thompson who revealed the role of women in Chartism in the 1830s and 1840s.

Stage 3: ***feminist/women-centred*** history – included a transfer of focus from the subjects deemed important by traditional, male-orientated history, to those of particular relevance to the lives of women. For example, the history of contraception, which is of peripheral interest in traditional male-dominated histories, might now take centre stage. The last quarter of the twentieth century saw a plethora of publications exploring 'new' avenues of history, such as Reay Tannahill's *Food in History* (1973) and her companion volume,

THINK LIKE AN HISTORIAN

1. To what extent is it important for a reader to know the sex of the author?

2. For what reasons, according to Thirsk, is the history written by women likely to be different from that written by men?

FOR DISCUSSION

In a small group, consider the following:

1. To what extent do you agree with Thirsk's comment on women and female historians?

2. Would a male historian have been likely to make the same statement?

Feminist/women-centred history

'… above all else, it is about the everyday experience of women, just as feminism itself is' (Sayer (1994), p. 7).

THINK LIKE AN HISTORIAN

How does 'feminist history' differ from 'women's history'?

FOR DISCUSSION

In a small group, consider the following:

To what extent can men write from a feminist perspective? If they can, is there such a thing as a 'feminist perspective'? If not, must historical interpretation always produce debate created by gender?

FOR DISCUSSION

In a small group, consider the following:

It is often said that we can learn from the past. What lesson is learned through the study of gender roles in history?

THINK LIKE AN HISTORIAN

Why might an historian contest the view that witch-hunting was sexually motivated and an expression of male violence against women?

Sex in History (1980). More conventional subjects, such as the industrial revolution, were now written about in relation to their impact upon the lives of women. Hence the emergence of titles like Jane Rendell's *Women in an Industrialising Society: England 1750–1880* (1990).

Since the 1970s, universities have offered women's studies courses. Modern studies have focused on the differences of the experiences of women in historical situations and how these were influenced by such factors as their race, class, religion and sexuality. Historians of the lives of women have come to focus particularly upon the central issue of gender which, unlike biological sex, is a social construct, and changing roles across time and place. Gender studies focus on how the lives of men and women are formed by the societies in which they live. Restricted opportunities and cultural assumptions are identified as key elements in their life experience and the forming of their mentalities.

Feminist historians of witch-hunting have focused on gender relations in their exploration of the phenomenon and found in these the root cause of the persecution. Anne Llewellyn Barstow, concerned with present and future gender relations, has drawn parallels between witch-hunting in the early modern period with modern forms of violence against women and pornography. Having catalogued certain instances in which accused women seem to have been subjected to severe sexual abuse by their interrogators, including intimate examination, sexual mutilation and rape, she has concluded:

> 'It appears that jailers, prickers, executioners and judges, all could take their sadistic pleasure with female prisoners. And so could respectable ministers and judges. At a public session in New England, Cotton Mather, while working to control a seventeen-year-old girl possessed of demons, uncovered her breasts and fondled them … These men took advantage of positions of authority to indulge in pornography sessions, thus revealing that they wanted more from witch hunting than the conviction of witches: namely, unchallengable sexual power over women … In the witch hunts, the policy of forcing a witch's confession may have been a cover for making a socially approved assault on her body … given the low opinion of women in European society, there was little social pressure to restrain the court officials from taking their pleasure with the victims.' (A. Barstow (1994) *Witchcraze*, pp. 132–3)

Stretch and challenge

Ask your teacher for a copy of the article in the teacher's LiveText entitled 'Women's history'. Write a summary of the evolution of women's history and an evaluation of its contribution to historical studies.

Conclusion

In response to the cynicism of Keith Jenkins and other 'postmodernists', Black and MacRaild have written a spirited defence of the theories in history that underpin historical interpretation:

> 'In general, it is not wrong to use theory in history. All thought is structured insofar as the human mind orders information in some way or another. Historians who claim to subscribe to no theory may in fact be said to be antitheoretical: that is their 'theory'. Theory grows from within the historian and is externalised as soon as he or she begins to select particular evidence. The quest for covering laws to explain historical phenomena such as the Industrial Revolution might seem either grandiose

or simplistic, depending on perspective, but, as Alex Callinicos (*Theories and Narratives*, 1995) has suggested, there is not a single historian who does not acquire understanding "inferentially by a process of interpreting data according to a complex system of rules and assumptions".

The postmodernists award ideas primacy in historical explanation. Since Marx, however, much more emphasis has generally been placed on materialist notions. The fixity of explanation that this implies (objectivity, truth, fact) has been challenged by post-modernists. However, too many of their criticisms are based on old-fashioned, stereotypical images of how historians work. In fact, the rise of Marxism, the *Annales* school of historians, and gender, social and cultural history have long since consigned the over-confident, narrow, male-centred and political focus of much nineteenth-century historical writing to the margins of what is now a wider and more vibrant discipline.' (Black and MacRaild (2000), p. 167)

This thesis reminds us that historians are very much the product of the age in which they live and of the political, social, economic and cultural climate of their time. Perhaps the most telling characteristic of any history is the language in which it is written. In the 1980s, a book for A Level students would be likely to address them as pupils and sixth formers; in the previous decade, historians writing such texts would be likely to politely indicate the titles of their academic colleagues, such as Miss Pauline Gregg, Mr A. J. P. Taylor, Dr Alan Bullock, etc. Just as language and its use changes across time so do the approaches of historians to the past. This is evident, for example, in the historiography of women's history outlined above.

A. J. P. Taylor, referred to earlier, was the great populist historian of the English-speaking world in the second half of the twentieth century. He was an exceptionally popular lecturer, a TV personality, and prolific writer of books, learned papers and newspaper articles. He wrote extensively about the history of the history he helped shape – that of the era of the Second World War – as an outspoken critic regarding the policy of appeasement, and as a member of the Homeguard. His initial writings about Germany in this period, such as *The Course of German History* (1945), were negative to the point of being Germanophobic. He considered National Socialism the natural product of a Germanic culture that could be traced back across hundreds of years. The triumph of Nazism was no mere conspiracy but the expression of the will of the masses. The same was true of the antisemitism that led to the policy of racial extermination. He was furious over the establishment of West Germany by the Allies at the end of the war and warned against the imminent danger of an emergent Fourth Reich. Such convictions perhaps should not surprise us. In the opinion of his biographer Robert Cole, 'He seemed to take Germany and the Germans personally, and perhaps what he had witnessed in this quarter century was justification' (R. Cole (1993) *A. J. P Taylor: The Traitor Within The Gates*, p. 75). As a socialist, he advocated a foreign policy that gravitated towards the Soviet Union instead of the USA in this period.

Taylor's great adversary over the origins of the Second World War debate was the right-wing historian Sir Hugh Trevor-Roper. Trevor-Roper is also associated with the historiography of early modern witch-hunting in Europe. His interest in, and views on this subject were greatly influenced by his experience of the Second World War. Raisa Maria Toivo has explained the links Trevor-Roper and others were making between the history of their own times and that of 400 years before:

'In the aftermath of the Second World War, with the experience of systematic genocide and totalitarianism, new developments in sociological and political analysis began to emerge, such as the logics of persecution and victimology. The history of ethnic minorities and of ideological crimes also assumed greater

prominence. As a consequence there was a general reassessment of the historical significance of the witch trials. The study of the persecutions both before and during the war and the study of early modern witch hunts seemed mutually supportive. Furthermore, in the post-war period the term "witch hunt" became a common descriptor for contemporary persecutions, such as the McCarthyite campaign against suspected communists and political purges in the Soviet Union.' (R. Toivo, 'The witch-craze as holocaust: the rise of persecuting societies', in J. Barry and O. Davies (eds) (2007) *Witchcraft Historiography*, p. 90)

In this case, the age in which the historian lived influenced both his choice of subject matter, witch-hunting, and his method, a comparative approach. Despite Taylor's arguments, the prevailing view at the time was that the persecution of the Jews was imposed from above as a political device by the Nazi leadership. The same elite, 'from above' explanation was provided by Trevor-Roper for the witch-hunts.

These examples reveal both how history is made and why it changes from one generation to the next. This is not something to deplore but something to celebrate – debate is the life-blood of the discipline; without it history would be as dead as the people it endeavours to understand.

Summary

This chapter has covered a wide range of historical concepts and theories and explored key elements in the formation of historical interpretations.

Key points

- *Evidence.* The fragmentary, incomplete and contradictory nature of evidence can result in a range of interpretations.
- *Historians.* The views of historians are influenced by such things as the time in which they are writing, their age, gender and creed.
- *History.* Modern historical writing comprises a great range of approaches and perspectives.
- *What is history?* Historians debate the meaning of the term 'History'. For some it represents the 'Holy Grail' of objective historical writing. For others, this seems to be an unrealistic and unattainable goal. Some 'postmodernists' have concluded that history *is* historiography.
- *Categorisation and classification.* History is in part, at least, the artificial construct of historians as they seek to bring some kind of order to the past.
- *Whig history.* The British historians of the eighteenth and early nineteenth centuries provided a positivist and triumphalist view of the past.
- *Chance in history.* Many historians have stressed the place of chance and coincidence in the shaping of history. Accident can be an important historical cause – an idea seriously at odds with structuralist or determinist approaches.
- *Structural interpretations.* Historians, inspired by social scientists, have explored the extent to which human actions are determined by social structures.
- *Historical determinism.* Social historians and sociologists interested in the past have hunted for the underlying historical trends in their analyses.
- *Profound causes.* Turner provided a profound 'Frontier thesis' to explain the nature of the 'American character' and its institutions.
- *Marxist interpretations.* Marx argued that a society's economic base determines its superstructure. His was a positivist interpretation of history that identified historic stages culminating in communism.

- *History and progress*. Most modern historians are less convinced than many of their 'positivist' predecessors regarding the optimistic view that history is essentially the story of human progress.

- *'From above' and 'from below' interpretations*. Debates in history sometimes revolve around the extent to which historical developments (cultural, political, economic, etc.) are determined from above by the elite or from below by the masses.

- *Psychoanalytical interpretations*. Psychoanalysis is now regarded as a weapon in the historian's armoury in the struggle to make sense of individual and collective actions in the past.

- *Feminist history*. Women's history has undergone important developments in the last half century. It has opened up new areas of research as historians have moved beyond the subjects traditionally studied and the questions traditionally asked by male historians.

- *Conclusion*. The subject matter, methodologies and interpretations of historians are determined by the age in which they live and write. Consequently, history is continuously changing despite dealing with an unchangeable past.

Historical approaches and methods

Introduction

The previous chapter explored the different interpretations of the past and it highlighted the importance of these different interpretations. Interpretations are partly shaped by the ways in which the historian investigates the past. Some of these have already been touched upon in Chapter 1 in the sections dealing with such concepts as Marxist history, gender studies and history from below. This chapter will develop your knowledge and understanding of the different approaches and methods historians have adopted in their study of the past and how these have developed across the last couple of hundred years.

The approaches an historian adopts are highly subjective and influenced by the historian's interests and own life experience. Historians are likely to approach the past 'at a different angle' from their predecessors and, in so doing, may well end up writing a very different account of that past. A 'from below' approach to the Crusades that focuses particularly on the role of women, for example, is likely to result in a very different kind of history to a more traditional 'from above' and male-orientated approach. One historian, studying the impact of the Norman Conquest for example, may set out to demonstrate how this resulted in fundamental changes in the way of life in England, whereas another may be determined to reveal how much of the old Anglo-Saxon world survived the invasion: they are likely to write two very different accounts of the past. Such concepts were introduced in Chapter 1 and they are further explored here as the evolution of modern history writing is explained.

The methods historians employ also shape the history they write. Some historians adopt a broadly scientific methodology by forming and testing a hypothesis. For example, an historian of British appeasement in the 1930s may set out to test the hypothesis that this policy was the outcome of structural issues. Another historian, however, convinced by the importance of the role of 'human agency' (i.e. individuals) in such matters might be less sensitive to the possibility that human actions are largely determined by factors beyond their control. Similarly, the Marxist historian, convinced that economic relationships are at the heart of history, is perhaps more inclined to carefully analyse statistical evidence for the crises in seventeenth-century Britain than the historian of religious radicalism. Some historians, such as those involved in studies of witch-hunting in early modern Europe, have adopted a method that takes a regional approach to the past and produced accounts, rich in local detail, that reassess the extent to which the experience of certain historical phenomena varied from place to place. Such alternative methodologies and their place in the history of history writing are further explored in this chapter.

Historical relationism

To a degree, modern historical approaches and methods have their origins in the Romantic movement of the late eighteenth and early nineteenth centuries. Ironically perhaps, historical fiction, specifically the historical novels of Sir Walter Scott, who strove to recreate faithfully the character and culture of the medieval world, were a big influence on the thinking of the most influential of the early nineteenth-century historians, **Leopold von Ranke**. Ranke, together with Barthold Niebuhr, was a pioneer of the approach known as '**genetic (or 'historical') relationism**' which championed the principle of exploring past events and individual actions in *relation* to past values and conditions. To this end, Ranke relied on primary sources 'to show what actually happened' (Ranke, quoted in Fritz Stern (ed.) (1956) *The Varieties of History*, p. 57). In so doing, he contributed to a new rigorous methodology that would remain the keystone upon which future historical writing would be based. For these reasons Ranke is regarded as 'the founder of the modern discipline of history' (A. Marwick (1970) *The Nature of History*, p. 38).

Ranke judged such things as memoirs far too unreliable. He was wary of the inclination to judge the past and considered it the historian's job to discover what happened in the past without passing judgement. Under Ranke's influence, by the end of the nineteenth century, historians had developed a systematic approach to their work. This has been summarised by Anna Green and Kathleen Troup as a three point process:

- 'the rigorous examination and knowledge of historical evidence, verified by references
- impartial research, devoid of *a priori* beliefs and prejudices [i.e. those based on a presumed historical 'law']
- an inductive method of reasoning, from the particular to the general' (A. Green and K. Troup (1999) *The Houses of History*, p. 3).

In Ranke's day history writing was, and perhaps still is, predominantly the history of political events. Considering the importance and drama of politics, together with the abundance of evidence for the subject, this is not surprising. The central importance of politics in history is summed up by E. A. Freeman's famous remark: 'History is past politics' (in J. Tosh (1984) *The Pursuit of History*, p. 67). The diplomatic history of modern times has received particular attention as historians have mined diplomatic archives to understand why catastrophes, such as wars, occurred. Public concern regarding the outbreak of the Second World War, and the debate regarding Britain's policy of appeasement in the 1930s, helped fuel the writing of influential historians such as A. J. P. Taylor, just as the recent war in Iraq is destined to merit the attention of future historians. Historians of English history of the seventeenth century are likely to focus their attention on constitutional developments in that epoch of change.

While Ranke focused on **'top-down' history** – diplomacy and politics – a Frenchman, Auguste Thierry, in writing his *History of the Norman Conquest of England* (1825) envisaged 'the destiny of peoples and not of certain famous men, to present the adventures of social life and not those of the individual' (quoted in Marwick, p. 41). In so doing he broadened the scope of history writing and laid the foundations for the social histories that appeared in the early twentieth century.

Top-down history

Studies of the past that focus on the evidence for, and actions of, the social elite.

History as a social science

The historian/proto-sociologist/philosopher Auguste Comte (1798–1857) identified history as a social *science*. He was concerned with the possibility that certain scientific laws fashioned human society. These laws, he suspected, not only explained the past but helped predict the future. As in the natural sciences, he advocated the forming and testing of hypotheses as the key approach to unlocking the truths of the past. This approach that links the 'social sciences' to the natural, or what Comte called the 'positive', sciences is termed 'positivism'. As explained in the previous chapter, positivist thinking was at the core of the work of the later nineteenth-century German political theorist and historian, Karl Marx. For Marx, the 'law' that shaped history was that of economic relationships and class struggle: 'The history of all hitherto existing society is the history of class struggles' (*The Communist Manifesto*). In the opinion of Arthur Marwick, the great contribution of Marx and Comte and their followers was that they inspired a new breed of historian: one that did not merely compile facts but endeavoured to explain their interconnections (Marwick, p. 45).

The Marxist approach to history is, essentially, a structuralist one. 'Structuralists' work on the assumption that the 'great men' of history were, like everyone else, the product of the environments into which they were born. Social, economic and cultural structures fashioned their politics as much as, or more than, their unique personalities. Consequently, **structuralist approaches** focus on these when explaining the major events of the past, such as the Crusades or the Holocaust, more than the individuals who helped perpetrate such things. Modern historians are as wary of ascribing past triumphs to 'hero' figures as they are of condemning 'scapegoats' for past calamities.

Narrative history

Whether or not they took on board Rankean ideas regarding documentation or subscribed to Comte's positivism, the historians of the nineteenth century were largely concerned with the writing of narrative history. Although this approach fell out of favour in more recent times, the establishment of a sound narrative remains a fundamental task of the historian. In its simplest form, history writing is story-telling, though the writing of narrative history is not a 'simple' activity. Historians, adopting this perfectly valid approach to the past, dedicate their time and energy to research the reconstruction of past events on the basis of the surviving evidence, all of which is limited and at least some of which is problematic. This activity is of particular importance for historians studying subjects for which the source material is relatively slight and the narrative of events is less certain. For medieval historians, their main business is likely to be the close examination of early narrative histories: the monastic chronicles. Every scrap of additional evidence, such as a law code, a list of fortifications or a property evaluation, is hugely important to the historian trying to verify the accuracy of the chronicles and 'filling in the gaps'. A chronological approach is often favoured by historians who are most concerned with political and diplomatic history.

Green and Troup have summarised the views of historian Allan Megill (1995) who distinguished certain categories or 'levels' of narrative history:

> '… these levels range from the micronarrative of a particular event; a master narrative which seeks to explain a broader segment of history; a grand narrative "which claims to offer the authoritative account of history generally"; and finally a metanarrative which draws upon some particular **cosmology** or metaphysical foundation, for example, Christianity' (Green and Troup (1999), p. 204).

The pre-eminence of narrative history has been overtaken in modern times by 'problem-orientated' history that is largely concerned with issues of causation. Not all historians have welcomed this development. Lawrence Stone in the late 1970s complained that the 'story-telling function [of history] has fallen into ill-repute among those who have regarded themselves as in the vanguard of the profession, the practitioners of the so-called "new history" of the post-Second-World-War era' (L. Stone, in Green and Troup, p. 210).

Literary and heroic history

Auguste Comte's contemporary, **Thomas Babington Macauley**, declared 'I shall not be satisfied unless I produce something which shall for a few days supersede the last fashionable novel on the tables of the young ladies' (quoted in Marwick, p. 46). Macauley's importance in the evolution of modern historical writing lies in his concern for its literary quality. Sometimes, as Arthur Marwick has explained, his laudable ambition of writing appealing, popular history took precedence over hard historical fact:

Structuralist approach

The assumption that the course of history is determined by structural factors such as a society's economic system.

Cosmology

A world view.

BIOGRAPHY

Thomas Babington Macauley (1800–59), Scottish Whig historian, poet and politician, wrote *The History of England from the Accession of James II* (1848).

'By the standards of historical scholarship established since the early nineteenth century, Macauley sometimes falls short as a historian. In his search after effect he sometimes cheated, his rendering of the past was less "truthful" than, given the resources available to him, it could have been. One notorious example of this is the passage in the first volume of the *History* ['History of England', 1848–55] describing the speech in which William III bade farewell to the States of Holland before setting out for Britain. Macauley writes:

"In all that grave senate there was none who could refrain from shedding tears. But the iron stoicism of William never gave way; and he stood among his weeping friends calm and austere, as if he had been about to leave them only for a short visit to his hunting-grounds at Loos."

Macauley had no reliable source for this fanciful description. In fact it is a direct plagiarism (conscious or unconscious) from the *Odes* of Horace, the description of Regulus making his farewell to the Senate.' (Marwick, p. 47)

Another very influential writer from this period, in Britain at least, was **Thomas Carlyle**. In his great moralising, polemical works he highlighted the roles of the 'heroes' of history. In so doing, he helped foster a vogue for history writing based upon the lives of the 'great men' of history that remains popular to the present day. Probably the most widely read history is biography. Individuals from the past such as Henry VIII and Adolf Hitler are of enduring interest and have inspired literally hundreds of books. By definition, biography provides a very singular way of observing the past. The 'great' men and women of history inevitably attract particular attention due to their high profile in their own lifetimes and the relative abundance of evidence they left to posterity. Sometimes biographers attempt to psychoanalyse their subjects. Much has been written, for example, about the significance of Hitler's vegetarianism, tee-totalism, and affection for children and dogs. Historians, however, cannot interview and observe their subjects on a psychiatrist's couch, and the paucity of evidence severely limits such approaches. The less available the evidence, the more the debate regarding an individual's personality is likely to rage. Medieval English kings such as John and Richard III have both their apologists and detractors. In any case, historians more convinced by structural explanations for historical events are less likely to seek solutions to problems in history in the personality traits of its leading protagonists. For them, '**psycho-history**' is a mere distraction.

THINK LIKE AN HISTORIAN

What are the limitations of history writing that takes the 'great man' (or woman) approach?

John Richard Green (1837–83) took a very different approach to the past to most of his contemporaries by emphasising social, as opposed to political, developments:

'The aim of the following work ['Short History of the English People', 1874] is defined by its title; it is not a history of English kings or English conquests, but of the English people … I have preferred to pass lightly and briefly over the details of foreign wars and diplomacies, the personal adventures of kings and nobles, the pomp of courts, or the intrigues of favourites … I have devoted more space to Chaucer than Cressy, to Caxton than to the petty strife of Yorkist and Lancastrian, to the Poor Law of Elizabeth than to her victory at Cadiz, to the Methodist revival than to the escape of the Young Pretender' (quoted in J. Black and D. MacRaild (2000) *Studying History*, p. 58).

BIOGRAPHY

Thomas Carlyle
(1795–1881), Scottish essayist and historian, wrote *On Heroes and Hero Worship and the Heroic in History* (1841).

Psycho-history

The application of the science of psychoanalysis to historical studies (see Chapter 1, page 18).

Is History a science?

By the start of the twentieth century, historians confidently asserted that 'history is a science, no less and no more' (J. B. Bury, 1902, quoted in Marwick, p. 55). Historical sources, in their opinion, needed to be approached with scientific rigour, laws shaped the past, and, as in the natural sciences, the truth of the past could be discovered. Lord Acton, Regius Professor of Modern History at Cambridge (1895–1902), commented, optimistically:

> '… the long conspiracy against the knowledge of truth has been practically abandoned, and competing scholars all over the civilised world are taking advantage of the change … [aiming to] meet the scientific demand for completeness and certainty' (from a note sent to the contributors of 'The Cambridge Modern History' in 1896, quoted in D. Aldred (1984) *Is History a Science?*).

In the following passages, J. B. Bury, Lord Acton's successor as Regius Professor, outlines the case for the scientific approach to the past.

> 'It has not yet become superfluous to insist that history is a science, no less and no more …
>
> All truths (to modify a saying of Plato) require the most exact methods; and closely connected with the introduction of a new method was the elevation of the standard of truth. The idea of a scrupulously exact conformity to facts was fixed, refined and canonised; and the critical method was one of the means to secure it. There was indeed no historian since the beginning of things who did not profess that his sole aim was to present to his readers untainted and unpainted truth. But the axiom was loosely understood and interpreted, and the notion of truth was elastic.
>
> … So long as history was regarded as an art, the sanctions of truth and accuracy could not be severe.
>
> … Though we may point to individual writers who had a high ideal of accuracy at various ages, it was not till the scientific period began that laxity in representing facts, came to be branded as criminal.
>
> And here … I may remind you that history is not a branch of literature. The facts of history, like the facts of geology or astronomy, can supply material for literary art; for manifest reasons they lend themselves to artistic representation far more readily than those of the natural sciences; but to clothe the story of human society in a literary dress is no more the part of an historian as an historian, than it is the part of an astronomer as an astronomer to present in an artistic shape the story of the stars.
>
> … The national movements of Europe not only raised history into prominence and gave a great impulse to its study, but also partially disclosed where the true practical importance of history lies.
>
> … It is of vital importance for citizens to have a true knowledge of the past and to see it in a dry light, in order that their influence on the present and future may be exerted in right directions. For, as a matter of fact, the attitude of men to the past has at all times been a factor in forming their political opinions and determining the course of events …
>
> It seems inevitable that … the place which history occupies in national education will grow larger and larger. It is therefore of supreme moment that the history which is taught should be true, and that can be attained only through the discovery, collection, classification and interpretation of facts – through scientific research …

We want … recognition that it is a matter of public concern to promote the scientific study of any branch of history that any student is anxious to pursue. Some statesmen would acknowledge this; but in a democratic state they are hampered by the views of unenlightened taxpayers …

… The Universities themselves have much to do; they have to recognise more fully and clearly and practically and preach more loudly and assiduously that the advancement of research in history, as in other sciences, is not a luxury … but is a pressing need, a matter of inestimable concern to the nation and the world.

Beyond its value as a limiting controlling conception, the idea of the future development of man has also a positive importance. It furnishes in fact the justification of much of the laborious historical work that has been done and is being done today. The gathering of materials bearing upon minute local events … the patient drudgery in archives of states and municipalities, all the microscopic research that is carried on by armies of toiling students … this work, the hewing of wood and the drawing of water, has to be done in faith – in the faith that a complete assemblage of the smallest facts of human history will tell in the end. The labour is performed for posterity – for remote posterity …

… Every individual who is deeply impressed with the fact that man's grasp of his past development helps to determine his future development, and who studies history as a science not as a branch of literature, will contribute to form a national conscience that true history is of supreme importance, that the only way to true history lies through scientific research, and that in promoting and prosecuting such research we are not indulging in a luxury but doing a thoroughly practical work and performing a great duty to posterity …

I may conclude by repeating that … if, year by year, history is to become a more and more powerful force for stripping the bandages of error from the eyes of men, for shaping public opinion and advancing the cause of intellectual and political liberty, she will best prepare her disciples … but by remembering always that, though she may supply material for literary art or philosophical speculation, she is herself simply a science, no less and no more .' (J. B. Bury, 1902, quoted in F. Stern (ed.) (1970), *The Varieties of History*, pp. 210–23)

THINK LIKE AN HISTORIAN

1. How does Bury define 'History' and 'Science'?
2. In what ways does Bury seek to demonstrate that History is a science?
3. Can historians reconstruct past events as 'scientific' certainties? Explain your answer.
4. Is History a science? Explain your answer.
5. How does Bury justify the study of history?

In 1903, the well-known, early twentieth-century British historian, **George Macauley Trevelyan**, Macauley's grand-nephew, taking the 'history as art/literature' position, wrote a sturdy riposte to Bury's claims that history is a science:

'The last fifty years have witnessed great changes in the management of Clio's temple [Clio – the Greek goddess (muse) of History]. Her inspired prophets and bards have passed away and been succeeded by the priests of an established church; … doctrine has been defined; … and the tombs of the aforesaid prophets have been duly blackened by the new hierarchy. While these changes were in

BIOGRAPHY

G. M. Trevelyan (1876–1962), like all historians, was influenced by the values of the age in which he was writing. He proved to be a keen advocate of the nationalist spirit in his *Garibaldi's Defence of the Roman Republic* (1907) – a stance that would fall into disrepute as Italy and other countries suffered the consequences of overtly nationalistic government. His *English Social History* (1944) appears to have been written as a patriotic gesture as the storm-clouds grew over Europe in the years leading up to the Second World War.

process the statue of the Muse was seen to wink an eye. Was it in approval, or in derision? Two generations back, history was a part of our national literature, written by persons moving at large in the world of letters or politics … Of recent years the popular influence of history has greatly diminished. History was, by her own friends, proclaimed a 'science' for specialists, not 'literature' for the common reader of books.

… Until quite recent times, from the days of Clarendon down through Gibbon, Carlyle and Macaulay to Green and Lecky, historical writing was not merely the mutual conversation of scholars with one another, but was the means of spreading far and wide a love and knowledge of history, an elevated and critical patriotism and certain qualities of mind and heart. But all that has been stopped, and an attempt has been made to drill us into so many Potsdam Guards [reference to German scientific historians – Niebuhr, Ranke and Hegel] of learning.

The functions of physical science are mainly two. Direct utility in practical fields; and in more intellectual fields the deduction of laws of "cause and effect". Now history can perform neither of these functions.

In the first place it has no practical utility like physical science. No-one can buy a knowledge of history, however profound, invent the steam-engine, or light a town, or cure cancer, or make wheat grow near the Arctic Circle. For this reason there is not in the case of history, as there is in the case of physical science, any utilitarian value at all in the accumulation of knowledge by a small number of students.

In the second place history cannot, like physical science, deduce causal laws of general application. All attempts have failed to discover laws of "cause and effect" which are certain to repeat themselves in the institutions and affairs of men.

The law of gravitation may be scientifically proved because it is universal and simple. But the historical law that starvation brings on revolt is not proved; indeed the opposite statement, that starvation leads to abject submission, is equally true in the light of past events … An historical event cannot be isolated from its circumstances, any more than the onion from its skins, because an event is itself nothing but a set of circumstances, none of which will ever recur.

To bring the matter to the test, what are the "laws" which historical "science" has discovered in the last forty years, since it cleared the laboratory of those wretched "literary historians"?

… Not only can no causal laws of universal application be discovered in so complex a subject, but the interpretation of the cause and effect of any one particular event cannot rightly be called "scientific". The collection of facts, the weighing of evidence as to what events happened, are in some sense scientific; but not so the discovery of the causes and effects of those events. In dealing even with an affair of which the facts are so comparatively well known as those of the French Revolution, it is impossible accurately to examine the psychology of twenty-five million different persons, of whom – except a few hundreds or thousands – the lives and motives are buried in the black night of the utterly forgotten. No-one, therefore, can ever give a complete or wholly true account of the causes of the French Revolution. But several imperfect readings of history are better than none at all; and he will give the best interpretation who, having discovered and weighed all the important evidence obtainable, has the largest grasp of intellect, the warmest human sympathy, the highest imaginative powers. Carlyle, at least in his greatest work, fulfilled the last two conditions …

I conclude, therefore, that the analogy of physical science has misled many historians during the last thirty years right away from the truth about their profession. There is no utilitarian value in knowledge of the past, and there is no way of scientifically deducing causal laws about the action of human beings in the mass. In short, the value of history is not scientific. Its true value is educational. It can educate the minds of men by causing them to reflect on the past. If historians neglect to educate the public, if they fail to interest it intelligently in the past, then all their historical learning is valueless except in so far as it educates themselves. What then, are the various ways in which history can educate the mind?

The first, or at least the most generally acknowledged educational effect of history, is to train the mind of the citizen into a state in which he is capable of taking a just view of political problems. But, even in this capacity, history cannot prophesy the future.

… History should not only remove prejudice, it should breed enthusiasm. To many it is an important source of the ideas that inspire their lives. With the exception of a few creative minds, men are too weak to fly by their own unaided imagination beyond the circle of ideas that govern the world in which they are placed … One may aspire to the best characteristics of a man of Athens or a citizen of Rome; a Churchman of the twelfth century, or a Reformer of the sixteenth; a Cavalier of the old school, or a Puritan of the Independent party; a Radical of the time of Castlereagh, or a public servant of the time of Peel … Another educative function of history is to enable the reader to comprehend the historical aspect of literature proper … For example, the last half dozen stanzas of Browning's "Old Pictures in Florence", the fifth stanza of his "Lovers' Quarrel" and half his wife's best poems are already meaningless unless we know something of the continental history of that day.

The value and pleasure of travel, whether at home or abroad, is doubled by a knowledge of history.

In this vexed question whether history is an art or a science, let us call it both or call it neither. For it has an element of both. It is not in guessing at historical "cause and effect" that science comes in; but in collecting and weighing evidence as to facts …

To my mind, there are three distinct functions of history, that we may call the scientific, the imaginative or speculative, and the literary. First comes what we may call the scientific, if we confine the word to this narrow but vital function, the day-labour that every historian must well and truly perform if he is to be a serious member of his profession – the accumulation of facts and the sifting of evidence … Then comes the imaginative or speculative, when he plays with the facts that he has gathered, selects and classifies them, and makes his guesses and generalisations. And last, but not least comes the literary function, the exposition of the results of science and imagination in a form that will attract and educate our fellow-countrymen. For this last process I use the word literature.

… Writing history well is no child's play. The rounding of every sentence and of every paragraph has to be made consistent with a score of facts … some of them perhaps discovered or remembered by him at the last moment to the entire destruction of some carefully erected artistic structure. In such cases there is an undoubted temptation to the artist to neglect such small, inconvenient pieces of truth. That, I think, is the one strong point in the scholar's outcry against "literary history", but … in history, as it is now written, art is sacrificed to science ten times for every time that science is sacrificed to art …

If, as we have so often been told with such glee, the days of "literary history" have gone never to return, the world is left the poorer … but if we confess that we lack something, and cease to make a merit of our chief defect, if we encourage the rising generation to work at the art of construction and narrative as a part of the historian's task, we may at once get a better level of historical writing, and our children may live to enjoy modern Gibbons, judicious Carlyles and skeptical Macaulays.' (G. M. Trevelyan, 1903, quoted in F. Stern (ed.) (1970) *The Varieties of History*, pp. 227–45)

THINK LIKE AN HISTORIAN

1. How does Trevelyan define 'History' and 'Science'?
2. In what ways does Trevelyan seek to demonstrate that History is not a science?
3. What, according to Trevelyan, is the purpose of historical investigations?

Social and economic history

In his not altogether successful efforts to write a social history of England (*English Social History*),Trevelyan is identified with the emergence of social history as an academic discipline in its own right. To the dismay of subsequent social historians, he defined social history as 'history with the politics left out' (quoted in Black and MacRaild, p. 59). Social history provided an alternative approach to the events-led view of the past.

The rise of the labour movement and socialism stimulated a new interest in the lives of ordinary working people. Their contribution to, and exploitation by, the economic systems they enabled, became valid subjects for a new generation of left-wing historians. The great pioneers of this approach in Britain were the social reformers, Sidney and Beatrice Webb, who founded the **London School of Economics** in 1895. In 1894, they published their influential *History of Trade Unionism*, which was followed by *Industrial Democracy* in 1897. In the USA, such approaches were termed the 'New History'. More recently, these approaches have become known as 'history from below'. Where, traditionally, the major developments of the past were deemed to be the consequence of the initiatives of the elite and the ruling class, modern historians are likely to identify popular culture as a crucial factor. 'From above' and 'from below' factors set the parameters of debate for many subjects, including the Holocaust, witch-hunting, appeasement in the 1930s and the Crusades. The changing nature of society has often been linked to political development; the crises of the seventeenth century in England, for example, are associated with the rise of the gentry and the political tension that ensued.

At much the same time, economic histories appeared, notably *War and Capitalism* by a German historian, Werner Sombart, in 1913. This explored the role of war in the process of industrialisation. The most influential early advocate of using statistics in the pursuit of historical truths, such as the standard of living in industrialised Britain, was the English historian, J. H. Clapham (1873–1946). The recognition of the place of counting in historical studies gave rise to a new journal, *The Economic History Review*, first published in 1926. In another age of great technological progress, the 1950s and 1960s, a 'new' economic history emerged, sometimes termed as 'econometrics or 'cliometrics' (after Clio, the muse of History in Greek mythology).

A further alternative to the nineteenth-century diplomatic and constitutional histories was the emerging 'intellectual history' of the new century, evident in the titles of such works as Friedrich Meinecke's *The Doctrine of Raison d'État and its Place in Modern History* (1924). Many historians, subsequently, have emphasised the importance of ideas in the past. Religion was, of course, the focus of the Crusades, and belief in the possibility of people making pacts with the devil seems to have helped generate the witch-hunts of the early modern period. However, historians with a more 'materialistic' perspective debate the extent to which ideas can override circumstances in the shaping of history. Researchers interested in the influence of ideas have to grapple with the fact that, until recent times, writings indicating philosophical understanding for any given period were usually produced by members of the social elite. It would be unwise, for example, to assume that the German Jesuit priests who wrote the most famous witch-hunting manual 'Malleus Maleficarum' in the fifteenth century accurately reflected the common mores of the age in which they lived.

In the following passage Arthur Marwick offered some interesting explanations for the appearance of new approaches to history in the early twentieth century.

> 'It may seem strange that historical studies in the early years of the twentieth century should simultaneously try to face in two different directions: in the direction of economics and in the direction of ideas … However, this turning in different directions was all part of the same internal revolution within historical studies: the bad old men of the dying generation had ignored both economic and intellectual factors, so the brave young men of the present must explore one or other or both. The turning to economic history, which had its origins deep in the nineteenth century, obviously makes sense in the context of a developing technological civilisation. The fashion for intellectual history was essentially a more temporary one, associated with the tide of philosophical doubt which swept the Western world in the aftermath of the First World War, washing away much of the older faith in the existence of solid historical "facts". "Everything is relative" and "It's all in the mind, anyway" were the cant phrases which affected and reflected thinking at all levels of intellectual activity.' (Marwick (1970), pp. 72–4)

THINK LIKE AN HISTORIAN

To what extent, and for what reasons, are historians' approaches a product of the age in which they live?

The Annalists

In 1929, two French historians, Marc Bloch and Lucien Febvre, launched a new journal entitled *Annales d'histoire sociale et économique*. In it they championed a broader vision of history, later dubbed '**total history**' or, more recently, 'holistic history' (Jordanova 2006) that tapped into the associated disciplines of geography, psychology, economics and sociology. They helped initiate an academic culture of integration across subjects. It is not unusual now for sociologists and social-psychologists to write texts on such historical topics as sixteenth- and seventeenth-century witch-hunting. The 'Annalists', as they came to be called, contested the traditional preoccupation with political narrative and the history of 'great men'. Sometimes they tackled a long time-span (*'longue durée'*) in order to identify historical developments that occurred over long periods of time. In trying to explain why things happened they sought 'profound causes' and considered such things as geography and climate upon the actions of men. Theirs was likely to be a macro, as opposed to a micro, history. This approach is exemplified in the title of their most famous publication – Marc Bloch's *Feudal Society* (1940).

Total history

A broad vision of history, associated with the Annalists school of historians, that tapped into the associated disciplines of geography, psychology, economics and sociology.

The history of the mentalities

Another great contribution of the Annalists was their recognition of the importance of understanding the '*mentalité*' of people in the past. John Tosh has explained how the history of collective mentality is distinct from the history of ideas:

> '... while the history of ideas deals with formally articulated principles and ideologies, the history of mentality is concerned with the emotional, the instinctive and the implicit – areas of thought which often have found no direct expression at all. And it is social historians rather than intellectual historians who have made the running in this new field.' (Tosh (1984), p. 86).

THINK LIKE AN HISTORIAN

Write a one-sentence definition for each of the terms 'social historian' and 'intellectual historian'.

The Annalists argued that, in terms of people's ideas and emotions, the past was indeed a foreign place. The collective mentality of the past was the product of specific time and place and it would be naïve to assume that people in the past shared the same psychological make-up of people in the present. Gaining access to the 'collective mentality', however, is difficult for any but the most literate of societies. However, it is sometimes possible, even when the people concerned wrote no record of their own. A more recent exponent of Annalist values, Emmanual Le Roy Ladurie, wrote an immensely influential book, *Montaillou* (1978) that reconstructed the lives of around 250 people living in a village in the Pyrenees between 1294 and 1324. His account was based upon the court records of the local bishop, Jacques Fournier, subsequently Pope Benedict XII, who kept the detailed records of the Inquisition which was investigating the **Albigensian heresy** in the region during that period. This 'micro-historic' approach has been much emulated. Ladurie's work was anticipated a few years earlier by Alan Macfarlane's *Witchcraft in Tudor and Stuart England* (1970), which also used the detail of court records of two counties to explore the beliefs and experiences of people subjected to witch-hunting in seventeenth-century England.

QUICK FACT

Albigensian heresy. Also known as the Cathars, the Albigensians advocated beliefs that were deemed heretical by the Roman Catholic Church. Among other things, they maintained that the physical world was the evil creation of Satan. This theory would help pave the way for beliefs in 'diabolism' (people making pacts with the devil) and the witch-hunts of the early modern period.

Demography

The study of population. Those who study population are demographers.

The Annalists' 'total history', inevitably, focused on history 'from below'. Marc Bloch's famous works on the feudal system focused on the peasants instead of lords and kings, and Febvre's first great account of the French Revolution, published in two volumes, was entitled *The Peasants of the North during the Revolution* (1924). Inclined to the left politically, his writing was informed by the Marxist concept of the central place of class struggle in history. History 'from below' developed throughout the twentieth century, flowering in the 1960s, with a new enthusiasm for such things as women's history, oral history, historic **demography**, and labour history.

Local or regional history

The 'local' or 'regional' approach to history that investigates the past at a micro level is, arguably, more likely to produce a genuinely 'total' history than the ambitious projects of the first wave of Annalist historians. As Tosh has pointed out, local studies can shed a good deal of light on issues of national significance:

> '… as a result of the many county studies undertaken in recent years, historians now have a more sophisticated understanding of the inter-relationship between religious, economic and political factors in the origins of the English Civil War.' (Tosh (1984), p. 91)

As Emmanual Le Roy Ladurie demonstrated, communities with a relative abundance of evidence were worthy of special attention. Alan Macfarlane's examination of witch-hunting in Suffolk and Essex was so illuminating precisely because, for those counties, the record of trials was especially complete. Detailed studies of localities in Norman England for which substantial records survive can be used as a guide for the wider experience of conquest. Equally, local studies can reveal regional variations – the experience of British colonialism, for example, varied widely from continent to continent and place to place.

Marc Bloch emphasised the importance of the comparative and regressive approaches to history. Comparison is a central activity of the historian – all historians, to a greater or lesser extent, are 'comparativists'. At a micro level historians compare and contrast evidence to try to ascertain the 'truth' of the past; at a macro level they compare and contrast societies that might be far apart in terms of time and/or place. Anthropological approaches, for example, endeavour to illuminate the past through the study of human behaviour in societies that can be observed in the present, or have been observed in the recent past. For historians interested in the principle of historical 'laws' in the explanation of why things change, Marxist historians for example, the identification of the common experience of diverse societies is a fundamental approach in the testing of their hypotheses. This is sometimes described as 'universalising comparison'. Equally importantly, comparative studies can undermine the temptation of historians to generalise about the past. Historians of early modern witch-hunting have found in the detail of witchcraft beliefs and the scale of witch-hunting at a local level plenty of evidence to challenge the view that there ever was some kind of universal European 'witchcraze'; historians of the Crusades recognise the great diversity of motives that inspired those involved, just as each Crusade itself was a unique phenomenon. This, the opposite of 'universalising', is known as 'individualising comparison'. The two are not necessarily mutually exclusive: the historian is often concerned with trying to establish whether either the differences or the similarities 'outweigh' the other.

With a keen interest in such things as place names, folklore, linguistics and maps, Bloch was able to see how the past resonated in the present. He recognised how the evidence of modern customs, for example, could enable the historian to 'regress', to draw conclusions regarding the origin of such customs. This technique is especially associated with the work of modern archaeologists and anthropologists.

The importance of the Annales historians in developing new approaches to historical writing has been amply described by Black and MacRaild:

> 'In 1924 … Bloch published his seminal work – "The Royal Touch", one of the classics of this century. It is a study of *mentalités*, ideas and beliefs – a classic *Annales* subject area. In it Bloch examines a belief, held in France and England down to the eighteenth century, that the king could cure the skin disease scrofula ('the king's evil') just by touch. In three ways, 'The Royal Touch' was path-breaking. First, it did not conform to rigid periodic boundaries and crossed the traditional divisions

**THINK LIKE
AN HISTORIAN**

In what ways did the
Annales historians help
develop the ways in
which historians
approach the past?

between medieval and early modern where necessary. Secondly, it was perhaps the first truly comparative history. By using comparison Bloch was formalising what he believed to be the way forward for all history. Finally, it was a study of 'religious psychology', an attempt to give meaning to the dominant beliefs and actions of real people. As such it shattered the mould of standard political histories of the medieval period. At this time, Febvre too was developing his interest in ideas, plainly influenced by psychology. "Martin Luther" (1928), for example, was far from just a biography, but was, instead, a study of "social necessity", of the links between men and groups. The new trend was set.' (Black and MacRaild, pp. 70–71)

The work of the French Annalists represented a revolution in approaches to the writing of history and yet it would be many decades before its impact was felt elsewhere. In the following passages Black and MacRaild explain how and why the approaches adopted by historians can be regarded as being culturally determined:

'In America, the *Annales*, like Marxism have been taken on board only slowly and patchily. This has been explained by American historians' liberal approach to the past, which mirrors the … political culture of that country, and by the absence in America of the social chaos that has pierced European culture and self-confidence since 1914. In Germany, the *Annales* "mentalities" approach did not take off till the 1970s, although many German historians were preoccupied with the modern period and the cataclysmic events of 1914–18 to 1945, the rise of Hitler and the spectre of genocide.

In Britain, the pre-eminence of traditional political history (especially in the 1950s and 1960s) was tellingly discussed by Peter Burke, in "The French Historical Revolution" (1990). Britain at this time, Burke suggested, was a good example "of what Braudel [the most famous "second generation" Annalist historian] used to call a 'refusal to borrow'". Despite the importance of the major works by *Annales* historians, they were met by an underwhelming response in Britain … Prior to the 1970s, the *Annales* works were only rarely translated.' (Black and MacRaild, p. 82)

**THINK LIKE
AN HISTORIAN**

What factors determine
the approaches taken
by historians? Make a
list.

Cultural history

The Annalist inspired 'history of *mentalités*' is also known as 'cultural history'. For some, archaeologists in particular, 'cultural history' specifically identifies the 'material culture' of the past – the artefacts and artistic works that help to define societies. For most historians, however, it is seen as an approach that is concerned with the history of popular ideas. Intellectual historians have tended to focus on 'elite' ideas, such as those informing science and the fine arts, whereas cultural historians focus on the popular culture of the past. This covers all manner of things as diverse as the histories of leisure, food, pop music, sex, crime, and witchcraft. In their investigations, cultural historians combine social history, anthropological and sociological approaches when explaining past modes of behaviour. The author of the following extract argues in favour of this approach:

'The past, we are often told, is a foreign country. We may add that History is a passport that allows us to visit that country. The trip will necessarily be short, so everything that we learn has to be understood as just a small part of what actually happened. Our experience in the past will be fragmentary. Like any traveller, we have to avoid seeing what we expect to see, leaving behind our prejudices and pre-formed opinions. Since nobody can completely accomplish this, and we always perceive reality through the prism of our own experience, every successive visit to the past will reveal different things. This doesn't imply that we cannot make well documented and soundly reasoned History, only that the past continues to change as we change.

… This is where Cultural History makes its entry. Historians realise that one of the main problems in trying to understand the past is sometimes not what we do not know but what we do. This is only an apparent paradox. If we are studying a problematic question, let's say the United Kingdom's Appeasement policy in the 1930s, we know what happened afterwards (its ultimate failure and the outbreak of World War II and all the horror that followed), something that the people whom we are studying (Britons in the late 1930s) could not – and for the good reason that our past was their future. Our understanding of the past is fogged and distorted by the subsequent events that eventually resulted in our present, and we should be careful not to make easy assumptions, based on a supposedly superior knowledge, about our ancestors.

A good way to avoid this risk is to try to re-construct what people and different groups thought at the time and why; what was their relationship with others, the problems and things that surrounded them and in what was their perception of reality, of their present. Here is where History takes as much as it can from Sociology and becomes New Cultural History. Notice that this new approach does not limit itself to describing the ideas and conditions of the Past, as traditional Social History does, or the coining of great ideas and tendencies, which is the focus of traditional Intellectual History. What New Cultural history attempts is far more ambitious and difficult, and perhaps for this reason more interesting … it wants to know why people did what they did by understanding what they thought and how those ideas came into being. Be ready, for this trip is no visit to old ruins and yellowed documents but to our ancestors' minds … and your own mind.' (A. Cazorla-Sánchez, 'The New Cultural History – and you' in *History Review*, March 2008)

THINK LIKE AN HISTORIAN

1. What arguments can be made in favour of historians who attempt to place themselves 'in the shoes' of our ancestors (the 'empathetic' approach)? What advantages are there in this approach?

2. Explain what Cazorla-Sánchez means by 'the past continues to change as we change'.

3. What is 'new' about the 'New Cultural History' when compared with the approaches of social historians and intellectual historians (i.e. 'old' cultural historians)?

Psychoanalytical history

Sigmund Freud fashioned the modern science of psychology in the first half of the twentieth century, and this science has informed historical writing ever since. Febvre declared his investigation into sixteenth-century views on religion (*Le Problème de l'incroyance au XVI siècle*, 1947) an exercise in 'historical psychology'. In Marwick's opinion 'no historian today could discuss the French Revolution, or any similar topic without acquainting himself with the discoveries of the individual and social psychology' (Marwick (1970), p. 59). The application of psychoanalysis to the explanation of the past has been described as 'the most powerful of interpretive approaches to history' by historian and psychoanalyst Peter Loewenberg (Green and Troup (1999), p. 59). As an example Green and Troup have summarised a contemporary psychoanalytical explanation for the rise of the Nazis:

'Wilhelm Reich attempted to blend history, in the form of historical materialism, with group psychoanalysis. In *The Mass Psychology of Fascism*, written in the early 1930s,

BIOGRAPHY

Sigmund Freud (1856–1939), an Austrian neurologist and psychiatrist, is popularly identified with founding the science of psychoanalysis. He identified in the repression of one person or group by another an unconscious human defence mechanism.

Reich synthesized the theories of Freud and Marx. He argued that Nazism, like all political movements, was grounded in the psychological structure of the German masses, in particular of the lower middle class. This group was anxious due to their increasing poverty in the face of depression and German war debts. Lower middle class fathers were authoritarian, and able to sexually repress their children on account of the correspondence of familial and economic structures: that is, the family lived and worked together. These psychically damaged children therefore became submissive, and were relieved to rely on an authoritarian *Fuhrer* in later life. At the same time they craved authority, and so acted in an authoritarian manner towards those below them. This is, of course, a simplified account but it serves to show how Reich enriched his analysis of a concrete historical situation with psychoanalytic insights.' (Green and Troup (1999), p. 62)

'Psycho-historic' approaches have some validity in exploring the actions of groups of people. The 'crowd mentality' and 'mass psychology' that psychologists can observe in the contemporary world can help historians in their analysis of the behaviour of those that persecuted Jews in the 1940s and 'witches' in the 1640s.

THINK LIKE AN HISTORIAN

1. Which parts of Reich's interpretation employ the psychoanalytical theories of Freud?
2. Which parts of Reich's interpretation employ the 'historical materialist' theories of Marx?

(If this is your own book, use highlighter pens to identify each approach.)

New economic history

Post-Second World War approaches to history – the 'New Economic History' – relied heavily on statistical analysis and other methods developed by the new discipline of 'social science' – 'sociology' as it was termed by Augustus Comte in the mid-nineteenth century. As historians came to recognise the full importance of economic developments in the shaping of politics, more attention was paid to such things as prices and wages. For a time, it seemed to some that the computer would become the principle tool in solving the riddles of the past.

Some of these 'New' historians, 'demographers', chose to specialise in the study of data related to population studies (demography). Like the research historians who are occupied just trying to complete the record of past events, demographers are fully employed in their reconstruction of past-populations from incomplete and difficult evidence. Historians pursuing explanations for historical phenomena, such as early modern European witch-hunting and the settlement of the American West, have explored the significance of population expansion.

The history of the marginalised

In the twentieth century, many historians approached the past with the specific intention of recovering for posterity the history of minority and marginalised groups that traditionally have been largely written out of, or misrepresented by, history books. The 'New History' of the late nineteenth and early twentieth centuries was largely focused on the experience of ordinary working people. Since then, other marginalised groups have received a great deal of attention. For example, the history of black communities in predominantly white contexts has been much explored, and a fair amount of work has been done on the history of homosexuality.

'Gender history', according to Green and Troup, 'arose from women's dissatisfaction with their historical invisibility' (Green and Troup (1999), p. 253). The history of women has become commonplace in university degree programmes since the 1970s. Historians are now concerned, for example, with the impact of the Norman Conquest on the lives of women, and the role of women in the Crusades, British empire-building, and the forging of the American West. Women, so often confined to the sidelines in the most studied historical subjects of the past, take centre stage in some of the most high-profile subjects of the present, such as the European witch-hunts of the early modern period. Similarly, students of the American West are encouraged to pay as much attention to Native Americans as white settlers, and other minorities that were persecuted with the Jews in the era of the Holocaust have received attention. British imperialism is studied extensively from a non-British perspective. It is recognised that around one fifth of 'cowboys' in the American West were African-Americans and not the white stereotype of mid-twentieth century Hollywood movies.

The history of imperialism benefits from a canon of historical writing derived from the experiences of the colonised instead of the more usual traditional colonialists' perspective. The following passage outlines one such post-colonial perspective:

> 'At the other end of the postcolonial spectrum of historical writing are the subaltern studies historians of India who employ contemporary methodology and theory to re-interpret the experience of colonialism. The fundamental perspective of subaltern studies is very simple: "that hitherto Indian history had been written from a colonialist and elitist point of view, whereas a large part of Indian history has been made by the subaltern classes"…The subaltern are those of inferior rank, whether of class, caste, age, gender or in any other way. Arguing that Indian history had largely been written from the perspective of the elite, the subaltern studies historians reject the conventional nationalist history of India which "seeks to replicate in its own history the history of the modern state of Europe".' (Green and Troup (1999), p. 283)

Similar revisions of the forging of the American West were made by historians in the second half of the nineteenth century. Like Women's History courses in many British university departments, Native American studies are now delivered in US universities.

History and anthropology

Just as twentieth-century historians employed the approaches of statisticians and sociologists, they also harnessed the methodology and discoveries of anthropologists. The term **anthropology** was coined by the naturalist Françoise Péron in his study of Tasmanian Aboriginal peoples at the start of the nineteenth century. In trying to understand past *mentalités*, some historians have explored more recent and contemporary societies. The approach is of central importance to archaeology. However, just as archaeologists are aware of the danger of presuming that the lifestyles and beliefs of modern Australian aborigines have anything in common with their ancestors from 40,000 years ago, historians have questioned the validity of explaining witch-hunting in sixteenth-century Europe by drawing parallels with witchcraft beliefs in twentieth-century Africa. Although problematic, anthropology at least has alerted historians to the vast range of human experience and outlooks that are shaped by cultural and environmental factors, and historic processes. Commenting on the fascinating business of exploring different cultures in place and time, John Tosh has concluded:

> 'For historians encountering a past society through the medium of documentary sources there is – or ought to be – the same sense of "culture shock" that the modern investigator experiences in an exotic or "primitive" community.' (Tosh (1984), p. 87)

FOR DISCUSSION

In a small group, consider the following:

What parallels can be drawn between post-colonial perspectives and feminist perspectives on history?

Anthropology

The study of human beings.

THINK LIKE AN HISTORIAN

1. What are the main limitations of anthropological approaches to the study of the past?

2. What is the appeal for historians of anthropology's techniques and insights?

3. Could anthropological approaches have any relevance to historians of the Holocaust? Justify your answer.

Anthropological approaches to the study of witch-hunting in early modern Europe were pioneered by G. L. Kittredge in 1929 and more thoroughly explored by G. Parrinder in 1958. The major works associated with the approach are Keith Thomas' *Religion and the Decline of Magic* (1971) and Alan Macfarlane's *Witchcraft in Tudor and Stuart England* (1970). They drew on the findings of E. E. Evans-Pritchard's anthropological study of tribal life in Africa, *Witchcraft, Oracles and Magic among the Azande* (1937), to help explain the witchcraft and witch-hunting phenomena in the early modern era. Most importantly, the findings of the anthropologists raised the historians' awareness of the interconnectedness of material conditions and popular beliefs.

More recent historians, however, are less convinced of the effectiveness of an anthropological approach:

'… anthropology … is simply not designed to explain change over long timespans, arguably still one of the major objectives of the historian. Moreover, even early modern England was a more developed society than those which have traditionally formed the subject matter for anthropologists. It had a complex and increasingly dynamic economy, a complex social structure and a fair degree of social mobility, a developed church, and a developed state judicial system. One must express sympathy and admiration of Macfarlane and Thomas's approach, and for their major achievement in constructing a totally new perspective on the history of witchcraft: nevertheless, it is probably instructive that few historians have followed them in their pursuit of anthropological comparisons … comparing tribal societies studied by anthropologists in the first half of the twentieth century like is not being compared with like.' (J. Sharpe (2001) *Witchcraft in Early Modern England*, p. 39)

Conclusion

In their excellent guidebook for students of history, *Studying History*, Black and MacRaild summed up their chapter on historiography by citing Peter Burke's conclusions in *New Perspectives on Historical Writing* (1991) regarding the differences between 'Old' and 'New' approaches to history:

'History of the "traditional paradigm" is concerned with politics; the new history, which "has come to be concerned with virtually every area of human activity", is not.

Traditional historians "think of history as essentially a narrative of events", although new historians do not entirely dismiss the narrative form, greater weight is given to structures than was previously the case.

Traditional historians focus on "a view from above … concentrated on the deeds of great men", whereas new historians favour "history from below", the view of the common person.

Traditional history is shaped around documents (empiricism); new history draws upon a much wider range of sources, including non-textual types, such as oral and visual material.

Traditional approaches fail to account for a variety of questions which historians must ask, whereas new history does not.

The traditional paradigm stresses the singular power of the authorial voice, privileging the historian's objectivity and balance. New history, however, stresses the variety of voices and viewpoints in the past and acknowledges the subjectivity of the author.

Traditional historians have emphasised the uniqueness of their subject; newer approaches stress intellectual interplay through inter- and multi-disciplinary approaches.' (Black and MacRaild (2000), pp. 84–5)

Much modern academic history is as concerned with the history of the history writing as it is with the narrative of events. For example, much has been written about how nineteenth- and early twentieth-century views of the Crusades, in which they were perceived as noble, chivalric and romantic endeavours, reflected the age in which they were formulated. The nineteenth century was the great age of imperialism in which western Europe imposed its values and political systems upon other continents, and Europeans were generally convinced that they were doing the wider world a favour in the process. It was also a period when northern Europeans, in their art and literature, celebrated their medieval 'Gothic' ancestry. More recently, anti-colonial attitudes have led to a revision of the 'heroic' crusade tradition. All major subjects have generated books that are exclusively concerned with historiography.

The 'postmodern' preoccupation with historiography and how the views of historians are shaped by the age in which they write as much as, or more than, the history they write about, is a cause of concern to some. These concerns have been eloquently expressed by Richard J. Evans in an article entitled 'Postmodernism and the study of history' from which the following is an extract:

'In order to understand any aspect of history, it seems generally agreed, we have first to understand what historians have written about it. But what if that was all we needed to understand? What if the past itself was unrecoverable in any meaningfully objective sense, what if historians, instead of merely interpreting and reinterpreting it, simply made it up as they went along? What if, in other words, there was no difference between history and fiction?

This, or something much like it, is the argument put forward, with varying degrees of emphasis, by a growing number of literary theorists, critics, and indeed historians themselves, as they contemplate the discipline of history and how it is written and researched. The ideas they are advancing can roughly be grouped under the convenient label of "postmodernism". For most of the twentieth century, so the argument goes, we lived in a culture of "modernism", grounded in a strong belief in science and progress. In historical studies, this was expressed in the belief that history was a science, and used a particular range of theories and techniques to analyse the documentary and other remains left behind by the past in order to achieve an objective assessment of what happened and why.

… In the postmodernist world, meanings are shifting and uncertain, truth unobtainable, objectivity a meaningless concept … History, in other words, is ultimately not about the past, it's about historians.

… If we do not believe that we can establish the truth about the past, how can we for example refute the obnoxious exponents of "Holocaust denial", who deny that millions of Jews were killed by the Nazis in the Second World War? Moreover, if oppressed minorities want to improve their position in society, they are hardly going to do so by writing only about and for themselves: they are going to have to dissect the mechanisms and institutions which oppress them, and convince society as a whole that these should be changed. Some wide-ranging view of history, indeed some concept of objectivity, is necessary for this.

When we have discounted the more extreme statements of postmodernists about history, what is left? If we distinguish in this, as in other areas, between extremists and moderates, the answer is quite a lot. The postmodernist emphasis on culture and identity has given rise to a great deal of new and important historical work … In

**THINK LIKE
AN HISTORIAN**

1. What are the main strengths and weaknesses of 'postmodern' approaches to the past?

2. Try writing a one sentence definition for the term 'postmodernist history'.

the light of moderate postmodernist criticism it is no longer possible to maintain a simple view of economic or social causation in history, and this too is leading to a lot of rethinking of major historical topics. But postmodernism is not just relevant to traditional historical subjects, it has also redirected our attention to the marginal and the apparently insignificant, much to the benefit of historical knowledge. Finally it has forced all historians to think again about what they are doing when they study the past, and that perhaps is its most important contribution of all.' (R. J. Evans (1998) 'Postmodernism and the study of history' in *History Review*, December)

FOR DISCUSSION

In a small group, consider the following:

'There remains today a fundamental divide between historians who believe that one should first decide what questions require answers, then wring answers out of whatever material is available, however unsatisfactory, and historians who prefer to be guided by the available material and to ask only those questions to which the material provides well-substantiated answers.' (Marwick, p.56)

What are the strengths and limitations of the two approaches described in this comment?

Summary

This chapter has considered the different approaches and methods historians have adopted in their approach to the past and how these have developed across the last couple of hundred years.

Key points

- Historical relationism championed the principle of exploring past events and individual actions in *relation* to past values and conditions.
- Top-down history focuses on the evidence for, and actions of, the social elite.
- Auguste Comte (1798–1857) identified History as a social *science*.
- For Marx, the 'law' that shaped history was that of economic relationships and class struggle.
- The Marxist approach to history is, essentially, a structuralist one.
- The historians of the nineteenth century were largely concerned with the writing of narrative history.
- Levels of narrative history include: the micro-narrative, the master narrative, and the meta-narrative.
- 'Problem-orientated' history is largely concerned with issues of causation.
- By the start of the twentieth century, historians confidently asserted that history was a science.
- Social history provided an alternative approach to the events-led view of the past.
- The 'Annalists' contested the traditional preoccupation with political narrative and the history of 'great men'.
- Cultural historians focus on the popular culture of the past.
- Sigmund Freud fashioned the modern science of psychology in the first half of the twentieth century and this science has informed historical writing ever since.

- In the twentieth century, many historians approached the past with the specific intention of recovering for posterity the history of minority and marginalised groups that traditionally have been largely written out of, or misrepresented by, history books.

- Just as twentieth-century historians employed the approaches of statisticians and sociologists, they also harnessed the methodology and discoveries of anthropologists.

- Much modern academic history is as concerned with the history of history writing as it is with the narrative of events.

Historical controversies – British History

EXAM TIP

Historical interpretations are often identified by labels such as intentionalist, functionalist, traditional, pluralist, revisionist and postmodern. It is useful to be familiar with these terms but it is not enough simply to use them without an understanding of what they mean. When answering a question, you will need to show that you know how adopting a particular approach can lead to one type of interpretation while a different approach may offer another interpretation. You must also make sure that you consider the strengths and weaknesses of these different approaches and the interpretations they produce.

Fyrd

This was the Anglo-Saxon army, formed from the thegns who held their land by military service, and the peasants who were paid for two months' service. Thegns were well-armed, with helmets, chainmail coats, sword or axe, and horse; the peasants were lightly armed. The Anglo-Saxon army normally fought on foot.

Introduction

This chapter comprises four case studies based upon the following British History options available for examination in the OCR GCE A2 History specification B Unit F985:

1. The debate over the impact of the Norman Conquest, 1066–1216

2. The debate over Britain's seventeenth-century crises, 1629–89

3. Different interpretations of British imperialism, c.1850–c.1950

4. The debate over British appeasement in the 1930s

For each case study, there is a brief introductory commentary outlining the background to the range of approaches that have been taken to explaining the features of the topic being studied. This is followed by a series of extracts from the writing of historians and a few primary sources. This is not an exercise in source analysis and evaluation. You will need to consider why historians create different interpretations of the same events. The activities linked to the extracts and sources should help you to work on developing this ability to link new information to what you already know in order to account for different interpretations.

Each case study surveys some of the major interpretations that historians have suggested in the ongoing quest to understand them. Over the years, each has been, and continues to be, a lively subject in which new evidence, new attitudes, new approaches and new questions asked have all contributed to produce ongoing reflection and reconsideration by historians.

Case study 1: The debate over the impact of the Norman Conquest, 1066–1216

Introduction

Considerable historical debate surrounds the impact of the Norman Conquest after 1066, largely concerned with the extent to which it resulted in significant change from, as opposed to continuity, with Anglo-Saxon/Scandinavian features. This is particularly true for the issues relating to land holding, military service and the church.

The following extracts and sources focus on the period 1066–1100 but consider the main historical interpretations of the short- and long-term impacts of the Norman Conquest in the period 1066–1216.

When assessing the impact of the Norman Conquest, the first issue to address is what Anglo-Saxon England was like before 'the thin red line of the Conquest' of 1066, in particular the situation and circumstances in terms of land holding, military arrangements (such as the 'select **fyrd**'), kingship and government, and the organisation of the church. Such factors have obviously influenced the historical debates over the relative strengths and weaknesses of the institutions of the Old English state under **Edward the Confessor**.

BIOGRAPHY

Edward the Confessor was King of England from 1042 to 1066, and was the son of Ethelred (King of England 978–1016). Ethelred was a direct descendant of Alfred the Great, King of Wessex, so the royal house of Wessex was of ancient descent.

Source (A) The Kings of England, 1066–1216

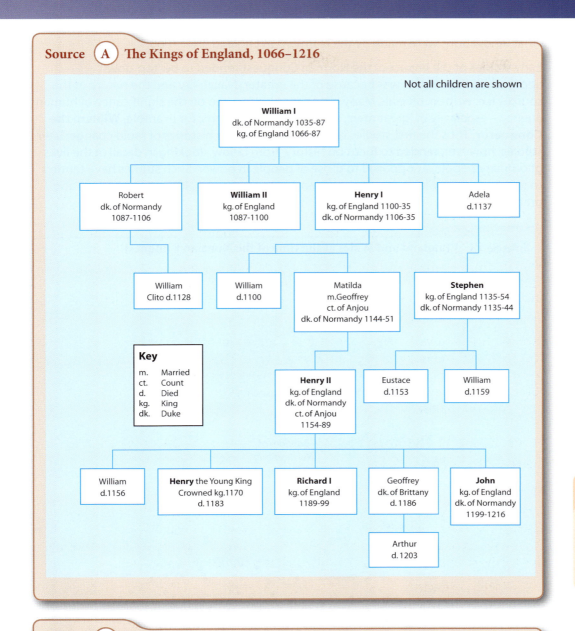

Not all children are shown

Charter

This was an official document which granted rights of authority.

Source (B) Village society at the time of Edward the Confessor

- At the highest level of village society was the thegn, who held the estate by right of **charter** ('book right') and had to do armed service, repairing fortresses and bridges in order to keep his land.

- Below the thegn was the geneat, a riding-servant or bailiff, serving the thegn in various capacities.

- Next was the cottar, who worked for the lord on Mondays and three days a week during harvest; he had five acres (two hectares) of his own land to farm the rest of the time.

- Below the cottar was the gebour or boor, equating to the later villein of medieval England. The boor was the main worker on the land, doing two days' work a week for the lord, sometimes three. He had to plough the lord's acreage, provide hunting dogs and carrying services and pay taxes, and at his death his belongings returned to the lord.

Adapted from the *Rectitudines Singularum Personaruml*, c.1042–66 ('The Rights and Ranks of People'), in T. Purser (2004) *Medieval England 1042–1228*, Heinemann, p. 9.

Which type of interpretation of, or approach to, the impact of the Norman Conquest does source B seem to support? Use your knowledge and understanding of English society just before and after 1066 to support your argument.

Feedalism

This was a hierarchical system of landholding based primarily on military service to a king or lord. Some historians argue that the social and economic bonds that tied peasants to manors must be included in the definition. Other scholars argue the term is so difficult to define accurately that it is best not used at all.

BIOGRAPHY

William the Conqueror was born about 1027. He was an illegitimate son of Duke Robert of Normandy who died in 1035, leaving 7-year-old William as heir to the Duchy. After more than ten years of internal and external struggles, by the 1050s, William had secured his inheritance and, by 1066, was the most powerful man in north-western Europe.

LINK UP

'From above' and 'from below' interpretations – see Chapter 1, page 17.

Narrative approach – see Chapter 1, page 6.

Narrative history – see Chapter 2, page 26.

It is also important to have some understanding of pre-1066 Norman society – especially of **feudalism**, the social structure, church and culture – in order to assess what innovations were made by the Normans in England after 1066.

Early studies of the impact of the Norman Conquest tended to be 'top-down' approaches. In part, this was because of the greater availability and the nature of the sources (i.e. written, official). Many historians also focused on the significance of human agency – especially of 'great men', such as the role of kings; for example, **William the Conqueror**. Thus the first studies tended to be narrative histories of rapid change; later studies, however, tended to focus on history 'from below', looking in detail at the lives of ordinary people, as opposed to those of people in power. Such studies have tended to show considerable continuity between Anglo-Saxon and Norman institutions and practices.

Source Ⓒ **England and Wales at the time of the Norman Conquest**

Passage 1 Continuity between Anglo-Saxon and Norman institutions and practices

Similar continuity is also the theme of those who attempt to analyse the impact of the Norman Conquest upon English rural society. Peculiarities in the structure of rural society in the late Anglo-Saxon period persisted, and the freedom of the Kentish and East Anglian peasants, the old-fashioned tenures of Northumbria and the Northern Danelaw, and the greater coherence of the manors in South and West England – to mention only the clearest examples – can be traced through medieval English history, and can still be identified as late as the sixteenth century ... In the field of institutions continuity is the essential theme of English history. The monarchy, the shire courts, the hundreds with their courts, the towns, the geld system of assessment and collection were all products of Anglo-Saxon experience and skill. The principal means and instruments of royal administration, the royal chapel, the solemn charter, and the sealed writ were familiar in late Anglo-Saxon days. The very coinage and system of weights and measures were convenient and fostered by the Norman conquerors. Only in their feudal attributes do the Normans appear as conspicuous innovators. Elsewhere it is as constructive builders on solid Anglo-Saxon achievements that their principal virtues find expression.

H. R. Loyn (1967) *The Norman Conquest*, Hutchinson, pp. 183 and 195.

What kind of approach to the impact of the Norman Conquest is taken by the historian in passage 1? How does the passage show this?

When examining developments in the study of the impact of the Norman Conquest, it is evident that changes in historical approaches have taken place over time. First, in the nineteenth century, a 'Whig' approach predominated, which tended to see the seeds of all later English freedoms in various aspects of the Anglo-Saxon age. Essentially, according to such evolutionist/continuity approaches, the Normans did little more than put fresh life into old institutions, while any 'foreign' elements were absorbed and assimilated. These 'Whig' interpretations are particularly associated with such historians as Kemble, Freeman, Green and Maitland, who saw history as the 'inevitable' progress of freedom and democracy – a similar approach was taken by Victorian historians studying the English Revolutions of the seventeenth century. In particular, they saw the military arrangements made by William I as being mainly adaptations from pre-Conquest customs. Maitland, a Victorian legal historian, though accepting that William I defined the amount of service due to him, argued against the idea that he had introduced any 'new principle'.

LINK UP

Whig history – see Chapter 1, page 7.

Passage 2 'Whig' interpretations of the impact of the Norman Conquest

The remarkable historical continuity and the even development of the political life of England have become a commonplace of history ... The evolutionist interpretation of the course of events governed the minds of Victorian historians like Kemble, Freeman and Green, whose generation did more than any other to dissipate the darkness which overhung the Anglo-Saxon people and their achievements. Unfortunately they could not escape the bias of their times, when British supremacy in the world was attributed to the beneficent workings of nationalism and democracy. Therefore, fully accepting the current perverse historical doctrine that the past could only be understood in the light of the present, they became preoccupied with tracing modern principles backwards. As a result, they were led to eulogize the Anglo-Saxon age, in which they detected the seeds of all later freedom, and contended that the incursions of the Normans did no more than put fresh life into the old institutions and intrude a foreign element which was absorbed and assimilated.

G. O. Sayles (1967) *The Medieval Foundations of England*, Methuen, p. 212.

1. Outline the main contributions of the approach identified in passage 2.

2. What are the problems associated with its methodology? How do they affect the conclusions drawn by using such a methodology and approach?

However, in the twentieth century, historical approaches and interpretations began to change. In particular, historians such as Round, Stenton and Douglas developed a new interpretation by placing greater emphasis on the influence of continental innovations, as a counter-balance to the evolutionist emphasis on continuity with Anglo-Saxon history. Round, for instance, saw the contractual arrangements between king and barons, barons and knights, as essentially a new social phase.

> **Passage** **Criticisms of the evolutionist interpretation**
>
> [This] cannot be said to point towards a uniform system of feudalism imposed by William the Conqueror on England after the Conquest. Instead, these documents show that different customs and different conditions were employed, depending on circumstances, in order to grant out the land … The extent and the timing of the introduction of knight-service and hereditary fiefs have been much debated. Towards the end of the nineteenth century, historians believed that the military arrangements that William I made were adapted from past, pre-Conquest customs. Accepting that William I defined the amount of service owed to him, the Victorian legal historian F. W. Maitland argued that 'it seems questionable whether he introduced any new principle'. But historians at the beginning of the twentieth century … saw the introduction of a contractual arrangement between the king and his **barons**, the barons and his men as a new social phase. R. A. Brown took this up in the 1970s and argued that the three fundamentals of feudalism were the **knight**, vassalic commendation and the fief.
>
> Purser (2004), pp. 76–7.

It could be argued that, in the attempts to emphasise the contributions of the Normans in the making of the English nation, the theories of cataclysmic and revolutionary change after 1066, resulted in a similar overexaggeration to that made by the evolutionists.

> **Passage** **A Scandinavian state in England**
>
> By 1042 western Europe, helped by an improvement in the climate, was beginning to recover from the last of those disasters which had kept it in poverty and ignorance since the collapse of the Roman Empire … The traditional cultural and political affiliations of England had been profoundly affected by the Scandinavian colonization of eastern England, eastern Ireland, and the Neustrian seaboard at the end of the ninth century. Hitherto, the Anglo-Saxon kingdoms had been in closest touch with those Germanic peoples which had created barbaric simulacra [equivalent] of imperial rule within the confines of the Roman empire … But the conquests and settlements of the Vikings, that ringed the northern waters, brought England fitfully within a Scandinavian orbit; and it was not until England was subjugated by the Normans, themselves of Viking origin, yet gallicized in part, that she swung once more, and finally, to face her southern neighbours …
>
> The unsuccessful revolts of 1067–71 completed the ruin of the English thegnhood … The uprisings led to **forfeitures** on a wide scale and to new grants to Norman lords. By 1086 only two Englishmen, Thurkill of Arden and Colswein of Lincoln, still held large estates directly of the king … The ruin of the Anglo-Scandinavian nobility was followed by the purging of the Edwardian episcopate … The widespread substitution of foreigners, especially of Normans, for natives in important church positions was doubtless inspired largely by political ends, although coloured by reforming zeal … The king cannot be blamed for this. Whatever may have been his original intentions or his early expedients, he had been driven by the events of 1066–71 to fashion a Norman state in his English kingdom.
>
> F. Barlow (1985) *The Feudal Kingdom of England, 1042–1216*, Longman, pp. 1–2 and 94–6.

Barons

This comes from the Latin word *baro* – by 1000, this was an old word in north-west France, and meant a man of status and quality, or a mature and experienced man. The estates of a baron were called 'baronies', but the term 'baron' was not a formal title at first – it was used to denote the more powerful Norman lords who were not quite of the status of the six or so earls.

Knight

This derives from the Anglo-Saxon word *cniht*, meaning 'riding servant'. Norman society in 1066 also included such a class of soldiers, distinguished by fighting on horseback – unlike the Anglo-Saxon fyrd – and by their loyalty to a lord. Knights were different from Anglo-Saxon thegns in that the knight's service was exclusively military, built around oaths, a code of loyalty and personal service.

Forfeitures

This was the loss of lands, offices or privileges, imposed as a penalty for wrong-doing or disloyalty.

Passage 5   Theories of a cataclysmic change after 1066

The disappearance of the Victorian illusion of progress meant the end of what had been little removed from unconscious propaganda masquerading as history and exposed to the scholars of the early twentieth century the aberrations of the evolutionist doctrine. It was not difficult to show the absurdity of these historical preconceptions and to tear them derisively to pieces. The new interpretation of the Norman Conquest placed a great emphasis upon the influence of continental innovations ... A highly coloured picture was painted of a completely decadent state, face to face with political anarchy and social disintegration and tied for its future to the culturally backward countries of the Baltic, and of a provincial and stagnant Church, cut off from communion with Rome and even the Church Universal. From all these evils, it was asserted, the Norman Conquest freed the country immediately by introducing Latin influences into State and Church in England for what is inferred to be the first time, thus bringing it into contact with Western Europe at a moment when the great constructive ideas, inherited from the Roman Empire, were coming once again to the forefront through an ecclesiastical reform movement and an intellectual and cultural renaissance. The evolutionist conception was thus displaced by that of a cataclysmic change, and the Conquest came to be openly regarded as a revolution which signalled the real starting-point in the unbroken development of England.

G. O. Sayles (1967), pp. 212–3.

However, later historians argued that both extreme interpretations tended to over-simplify, therefore offering only superficial opinions and explanations of the impact of the Norman Conquest. There has therefore been a more recent tendency to attempt a synthesis based, in particular, on detailed empirical studies, especially of local areas.

Passage 6   The debate about feudalism

The question is often asked, was feudalism introduced by William the Conqueror? What traces were there of feudalism in the time of King Edward? To these questions very various answers have been given, partly because historians have differed about the facts, partly because the question itself is ambiguous ... The Normans were extremely adaptable. They could destroy, but they could also pick out from the ruins valuable materials, and make with them buildings more elaborate than those they had destroyed. The Norman Conquest was a catastrophe; the Anglo-Saxon upper class was almost exterminated in twenty years ... Another question which is often asked is: did feudalism conduce to strong government or to anarchy? Such a question is not nonsensical. A governing class for whom warfare is a normal kind of exercise is not easy to control: a feudal society was never wholly peaceful ... Even in England, feudal anarchy flourished in the reign of **Stephen** *(1135–54). But the question itself can never be answered. No king ever ruled by feudalism alone; most of the problems of government cannot be answered in these terms ... The Anglo-Saxon monarchy survived, developed and strengthened by the Norman kings.*

C. Brooke (1965) *From Alfred to Henry III*, Nelson, pp. 105 and 108.

FOR DISCUSSION

In a small group, consider the following:

To what extent do passages 3, 4 and 5 indicate a modification/rejection of 'orthodox' evolutionist interpretations of the impact of the Norman Conquest?

Summarise the interpretation explained by Sayles in passage 5.

LINK UP

Local/regional approach – see Chapter 2, page 35.

Look at what passage 6 says about feudalism in England, and refer also to source B on page 45. Outline the main historical definitions of, and arguments about, feudalism provided by other historians.

BIOGRAPHY

Stephen of Blois was born around 1096, and was the younger son of Adele, daughter of William the Conqueror, and thus the nephew of Henry I. In 1131, Henry I's daughter, Matilda, was recognised as Henry's successor, but when Henry died unexpectedly in 1135, Stephen seized the throne. He ruled from 1135 to 1154, but there was intermittent civil war between the supporters of Stephen and Matilda, and it was her son who became king in 1154.

BIOGRAPHY

William Rufus was William I's second son and became King William II on his father's death in 1087; his elder brother, Robert, was duke of Normandy, and England and Normandy thus became divided again. His relations with the Church were not good. This, and the fact that he was almost certainly gay, resulted in the Christian chroniclers giving him a very bad 'press'. He died in 1100 and was succeeded by his younger brother, Henry.

Passage 7   Definitions of feudalism

Feudalism is an all-embracing term, which includes the large world of knightly heroes as well as the restrictive legalism of twelfth-century charters. In English history the different definitions can be built up on top of each other to mark chronological stages. Before 1066 England was a feudal society in the broad terms used by Marc Bloch. As a consequence of the Norman Conquest it became more rigorously militarised by the building of castles and the introduction of specialised knights. With **William Rufus**, *'that celebrated man, vigorous in knighthood', chivalric values are displayed for the first time. Then in the reign of Henry I the king's clerks and other drafters of documents begin to define services more exactly. This is when the term* feodum *meaning a 'fief' is first used in England. As a consequence, feudalism became institutionalised in the twelfth century as a system of holding property and raising revenue. Building on the powerful traditions of the Anglo-Saxon monarchy, the Norman kings thus consolidated their hold on England by heading a hierarchy of lords controlling knights and castles.*

M. T. Clanchy (1988) *England and its Rulers, 1066–1271*, Fontana, pp. 86–7.

Passage 8   Continuity and change under William I

William took over in its entirety the English administrative and judicial system, and left its operation very largely in the hands of the native magnates, officials and clerks who had served the Confessor. He naturally retained his own household and his own Curia, *or Council; but ... the number of Normans entrusted with rule was at first surprisingly small. They were intended to co-operate with the surviving English bishops, abbots and sheriffs, by whom they were greatly outnumbered. Even though the king evidently mistrusted the greater English nobles ..., he did not deprive them of their rank or diminish their honour.*

On the military side, however, William made a clean break with the past.

G. W. S. Barrow (1985) *Feudal Britain*, Edward Arnold, pp. 37–8.

1. What approach to the impact of the Norman Conquest is taken by the authors of passages 7 and 8? Write down specific phrases from both passages that indicate this.

2. Because both talk extensively about feudalism, is Clanchy (passage 7) concerned with a 'top-down' explanation?

Therefore, it now tends to be argued that 1066 should not be seen as the 'beginning of English history'. Instead, the period 1066–1216 should be seen as one characterised by a complex interaction and blending of two different systems of government, and two different structures of society. This resulted in a re-modelled and distinctive synthesis between Saxon and Norman.

THINK LIKE AN HISTORIAN

Re-read the case study about the immediate impact of the Norman Conquest, and work through the two questions that follow:

(a) What can you learn from passage 1 about the interpretations, approaches and methods of this historian? Refer to the extract and your knowledge to explain your answer.

EXAM TIP

When answering question (a), you will need to do *two* things:

(i) Support your answer by *detailed* reference to the extract AND refer to alternative approaches/methods.

(ii) Use relevant and accurate knowledge as part of a thorough analysis of the interpretation.

(b) Some historians have focused on a top-down approach to explain the impact of the Norman Conquest. Explain how this has contributed to our understanding of developments in the period 1066–1100. Has this approach any disadvantages or shortcomings?

EXAM TIP

As with (a) questions, you will have to do *two* things to achieve a top grade in (b) questions:

(i) Show both advantages and disadvantages/shortcomings of the approach/method, AND compare it with other approaches/methods.

(ii) Use relevant and accurate knowledge to assess both advantages *and* disadvantages.

EXAM TIP

Before submitting your answer to the questions above and moving on to the next case study, use the checklist below to make sure you have taken the right approach for a top grade.

If this is your own book, put ticks in the boxes as appropriate. Remember, the job isn't done until all the boxes have been filled.

Key areas checklist

Knowledge and understanding	Understanding of approaches/methods	Evaluation of approaches/ methods
To tick this box, you need to show/use some precise additional own knowledge about events and developments relevant to the topic, and show awareness and understanding of issues relating to the available evidence.	To tick this box, you need to understand the nature of the different approaches used by historians, and the reasons for this (e.g. personal beliefs about what history is, the influence of contemporary events, the type/nature of evidence available and the questions asked of it).	To tick this box, you need to be able to show you are aware of the strengths and weaknesses of the various approaches/ interpretations relevant to the topic, e.g. what can be learned from one approach that cannot be gained from others; how different perspectives on the debates provide different answers to the questions asked; whether the different interpretations can be combined to produce a synthesis.
Achieved?	Achieved?	Achieved?

EXAM TIP

In looking at different interpretations of the past, it is important to understand the reasons for these differences. You will need to ask yourself questions like those posed in this case study. As well as helping you to decide on your own interpretation of events, this should help you to understand how and why different historians have come to their conclusions, and how their alternative arguments might be supported and sustained. Equally, it should help you to point out any drawbacks and/or weakness in their interpretations.

The impact of the Norman Conquest: other aspects of controversy

Apart from the change/continuity and degree of change debates, other aspects of controversy include:

■ Whether the Conquest was colonial in nature, i.e. was there a Norman empire?

■ Gender issues related to the question of the impact of the Conquest on the roles and status of women – was the Conquest a turning point?

■ The relative importance of changes during the later reigns of Henry I, Stephen and Henry II.

Stretch and challenge

1. Identify for sources A–C and passages 1–8 issues relevant to (a) the nature of 'feudalism' and (b) the debate over this concept.

2. Why is 'feudalism' important to our understanding of Norman England?

3. Is the term a construct invented by historians?

4. What questions would you ask of the evidence to test further the validity of the concept?

Case study 2: The debate over Britain's seventeenth-century crises, 1629–89

Introduction

Considerable historical debate surrounds the various crises in seventeenth-century English – and British – history. This is particularly true for the causes and nature of the Civil War which broke out in 1642, and the interregnum period, 1649–60.

The following extracts focus on one of these crises, the period 1629–42, but involve consideration of the main historical interpretations concerning Britain's seventeenth-century crises.

The earliest accounts of the period 1629–60 were by contemporaries such as the Puritan and Republican Edmund Ludlow, who opposed both Charles I and Oliver Cromwell's Protectorate. He explained the Civil War as being the direct result of Charles I's attempts to establish a continental-style absolutist monarchy, and Archbishop Laud's attempt to destroy Puritanism in the Church of England. Of greater significance is the account given by Edward Hyde, the Earl of Clarendon. He saw the Civil War as resulting from a breakdown of relations between king and parliament in the period 1625–40, mainly as a result of an attempt by some men (notably Pym) who used religion as a 'cloak' to hide their political ambitions, to seize power and destroy the constitutional rights of the king. Clarendon's *History of the Great Rebellion* (published 1702–4) is the fullest contemporary attempt to chronicle and explain the Civil War from a conservative point of view. After the restoration of Charles II in 1660, historians tended to follow Clarendon's conservative approach in explaining the 'Great Rebellion'.

EXAM TIP

When starting to investigate different historical interpretations and explanations of the various seventeenth-century British crises from 1629 to 1689, remember to go beyond a 'labels/schools of thought' approach. Instead, try to examine closely the evidence historians have used, and the strengths/weaknesses of their interpretations.

Passage (1) **Clarendon's view on the origins of the Civil War**

*And no question, as the exorbitancy of the House of Commons this parliament hath proceeded principally from their contempt of laws, and that contempt from the scandal of that judgement [**Hampden's case**] ... who had always looked before upon [the judges] as the oracles of the law, and the best guides and directors of their opinions and actions: and they now thought themselves excused for swerving from the rules and customs of their predecessors (who in altering and making of laws ... had always observed the advice and judgement of those sages) in not asking questions of those whom they knew nobody would believe ... If [the judges] had preserved the simplicity of their ancestors in severely and strictly defending the laws, other men had observed the modesty of theirs in humbly and dutifully obeying them.*

Edward Hyde, Earl of Clarendon, *The History of the Rebellion and Civil Wars in England begun in the year 1641*, quoted in W. D. Macray (ed.) (1888), vol. 1, p. 124.

QUICK FACT

Hampden's case relates to a test case over John Hampden's refusal to pay Ship Money in 1637, which Charles I had begun to collect regularly after the dissolution of Parliament in 1629. Seven of the 12 judges ruled that the collection was legal, as the king alone could judge an 'emergency', but some of the judges' comments increased fears about royal absolutism which the Petition of Right had tried to address.

Source (A) **Events during Charles I's personal rule, 1629–42**

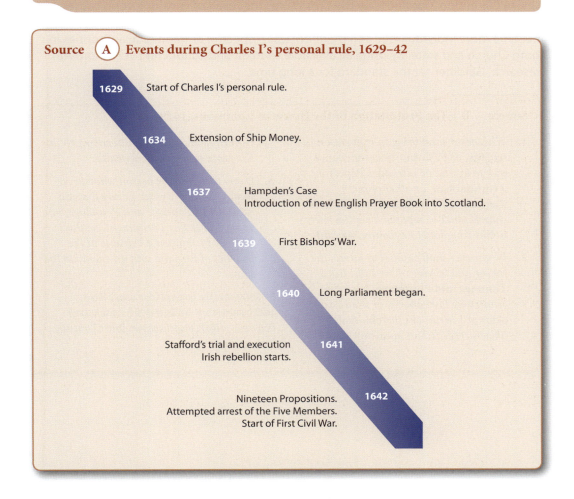

1629 — Start of Charles I's personal rule.

1634 — Extension of Ship Money.

1637 — Hampden's Case
Introduction of new English Prayer Book into Scotland.

1639 — First Bishops' War.

1640 — Long Parliament began.

1641 — Stafford's trial and execution
Irish rebellion starts.

1642 — Nineteen Propositions.
Attempted arrest of the Five Members.
Start of First Civil War.

How far do passages 1 and 2 support the view that the conflict between Parliament and Crown was:

(a) due to the personality of the king

(b) a struggle for political liberty?

LINK UP

Whig history – see Chapter 1, page 7.

Arminianism

An anti-Calvinist doctrine first put forward in England by Richard Hooker and Lancelot Andrews. It was based on the views of Jacobus Arminius, a Dutch theologian (d. 1609), and rejected strict ideas of grace and predestination. Arminianism caused great controversy among Protestants, and in England became associated with William Laud, whom Charles appointed Archbishop of Canterbury in 1633. Laud stressed the authority of bishops and 'High Church' worship with greater ceremony. What Laud and his allies were trying to do is as much debated as is the impact of their policies.

Passage ② Charles I: personality and views

Charles I is also a man of considerable contradictions and controversy. The Whig historians, notably Gardiner, portray him as sick in mind and essentially stupid, beneath a veneer of intellectualism and culture ... Charles had an aggressive, unsubtle self-confidence which had been encouraged, if anything, by his dealings with [those] Parliaments [of 1621 and 1624]. His were the politics of confrontation, not discussion ... He was not as vocal as his father about the Divine Right of Kings, but he believed in it more firmly, and was not prepared to compromise as James had been. James' beliefs, in fact, were largely a reaction to Scots conditions, and [in England] he was willing to qualify them. Charles took them over unaltered as a blueprint for the English constitution.

J. P. Kenyon (1985) *Stuart England*, Cambridge University Press, pp. 100–1.

In the nineteenth century, historical approaches and interpretations began to change. In particular, a 'Whig' interpretation developed which saw history as the 'inevitable' progress of freedom and democracy. Hence the Civil War was the result of an outdated feudal-style monarchy refusing to acknowledge the progressive attempts by Parliament to bring about a legitimate sharing of power, and a more democratic political system. Influenced by the various reforms in the nineteenth century (in particular the extensions of the franchise), most Victorian historians saw the history of the crises of 1629–60 as part of the slow but inevitable rise of Parliamentary democracy.

The main exponents of this approach were T. B. Macaulay and, especially, S. R. Gardiner. Unlike Clarendon, Gardiner saw the Civil War as the result of very long-term causes, both political and religious, resulting in a 'Puritan Revolution'. This led people to become more individualistic and therefore less respectful of traditional authorities in both Church and state. By using all available sources, and conducting very thorough research, Gardiner set the standard for a long time.

Source ⑧ The Protestation of the House of Commons, 1629

1. *Whosoever shall bring in innovation in religion, or by favour or countenance seek to extend or introduce Popery or **Arminianism**, or other opinion disagreeing from the true and orthodox church, shall be reputed a capital enemy to this Kingdom and Commonwealth.*

2. *Whosoever shall counsel or advise the taking and levying of the subsidies of **Tonnage and Poundage**, not being granted by Parliament, or shall be an actor or instrument therein, shall be likewise reputed an innovator in the Government, and a capital enemy to this Kingdom and Commonwealth.*

3. *If any merchant or person whatsoever shall voluntarily yield, or pay the said subsidies of Tonnage and Poundage, not being granted by Parliament, he shall likewise be reputed a betrayer of the liberties of England and an enemy to the same.*

Protestation of the House of Commons, 2 March 1629, quoted in S. R. Gardiner (1902) *Constitutional Documents of the Puritan Revolution*, Oxford University Press, pp. 82–3.

Source Charles I's views on the Petition of Right

As we have been careful for the settling of religion and quieting the church, so were we not unmindful of the preservation of the just and ancient liberties of our subjects, which we secured to them by our gracious answer to the Petition [of Right] in Parliament, having not since that time done any act whereby to infringe them;...

We are not ignorant how much that House [of Commons] hath of late years endeavoured to extend their privileges, by setting up general committees for religion, for courts of justice, for trade and the like; a course never heard of until of late ...

In these innovations (which we shall never permit again) they pretended indeed our

service, but their drift was to break, by this means, through all respects and ligaments of government, and to erect a universal over-swaying power to themselves, which belongs only to us, and not to them ...

We do also declare that we will maintain the ancient and just rights and liberties of our subjects ... Yet let no man hereby take the boldness to abuse that liberty ...; nor misinterpret the Petition by subverting it to a lawless liberty, wantonly or forwardly, under that or any other colour, to resist lawful or necessary authority.

Declaration of Charles I, published 10 March 1629; quoted in C. W. Daniels and J. Morrill (1991) *Charles I*, Cambridge University Press, pp. 31–2.

QUICK FACTS

Tonnage and Poundage were customs duties, normally voted for life to every monarch by Parliament at the beginning of each reign. This was not done for Charles I because of disagreements over his friend and adviser, the Duke of Buckingham, and foreign policy. However, Charles continued to collect it – this, in part, explains the petition of Right of 1628–9, and the later Protestation.

However, in the twentieth century, a new line of interpretation developed, influenced by Marxist approaches which tended to stress economic and social factors, and, in particular, the idea of struggle between classes. As regards the seventeenth-century crises, such historians tended to see an aristocratic feudal system, topped by the king, facing a growing challenge from a rising gentry or landowning middle class, increasingly represented in the House of Commons. The main proponents of such an approach were R. H. Tawney and, especially, Christopher Hill – the latter (influenced in part by the rise of fascism in the 1930s and the USSR's role in defeating Nazism in the Second World War) developed the clearest Marxist-based interpretation of the period 1603–60. Like Gardiner, he singled out Puritanism as a key factor because, he argued, it was linked to the individualism and the aims and interests of the rising gentry, with its emphasis on hard work and its belief that worldly success was a sign of God's approval. Hill's work in the 1950s and 1960s influenced many historians, including many who were not Marxists. Lawrence Stone, for instance, focused more on the decline of the aristocracy than on the rise of the gentry, as a factor in the outbreak of Civil War in 1642.

Passage A Marxist-based interpretation

The struggle for freedom, then, in the seventeenth century, was a more complex story than the books sometime suggest. The men of property won freedom – freedom from taxation and arbitrary arrest, freedom from religious persecution, freedom to control the destinies of their country through their elected representatives, freedom to buy and sell. They also won freedom to evict copyholders and cottagers, to tyrannize over their villagers, to hire unprotected labour in

the open market ... The smaller men failed to win either the vote or economic security ...

Freedom is not something abstract. It is the right of certain men to do certain things ... Only very slowly and late have men come to understand that unless freedom is universal it is only extended privilege.

C. Hill (1961) *The Century of Revolution, 1603–1714*, Sphere, pp. 310–1.

LINK UP

Marxist interpretations – see Chapter 1, page 13.

William Laud was rapidly promoted by Charles I, first as Bishop of London and then, in 1633, as Archbishop of Canterbury (Charles had promised him this post as early as 1626). Laud was a supporter of Arminianism and therefore unpopular with Puritans. In particular, he was opposed to the toleration (which James I had allowed) of those who did not follow all the practices of the Prayer Book.

QUICK FACTS

Possessive individualism was a seventeenth-century belief that a person was only a 'free-born Englishman' if he had sufficient property not to have to work for others. The latter were described as 'servants', and were held to have 'sold their birth right', and so were not entitled to a say in how the country was run.

In passage 4, what aspects of focus and language suggest the writer might be taking an essentially Marxist approach?

Passage ④ An interpretation influenced by the Marxist approach

There is little doubt that Charles I and **Laud** had dreams of erecting a continental-style baroque absolute monarchy, resting on the three pillars of arbitrary taxation, unquestioned acceptance of the Divine Right of Kings and an intimate union of Church and Crown. If they had succeeded, the fragile pre-war developments of ideas about **possessive individualism** would certainly have come to a grinding halt.

Hill and I are thus now in agreement that the English Revolution was not caused by a clear conflict between feudal and bourgeois ideologies and classes; that the alignment of forces among the rural elites did not correlate with attitudes towards ruthless enclosure; that the parliamentarian gentry had no conscious intention of destroying feudalism; but that the end result, first of the royal defeat and second of the consolidation of that defeat in the Glorious Revolution forty years later, was decisive. Together they made possible the seizure of political power by landed, mercantile and banking elites, which in turn opened the way to England's advance into the age of the Bank of England, the stockmarket, aggressive economic liberalism, economic and affective individualism, and an agricultural entrepreneurship among the landed elite ...

L. Stone, 'The bourgeois revolution of seventeenth-century England revisited', in G. Eley and W. Hunt (eds) (1988), *Reviving the English Revolution*, Verso Books, p. 287.

From the 1960s, there have been many more publications, several of which – to one degree or another – have modified the Whig and Marxist approaches. Perez Zagorin, for instance, in *The Court and the Country: The Beginning of the English Revolution* (1969), emphasised the way in which the royal court became culturally divided and cut off from the country gentry.

Source ⒟ Economic and social developments, 1550–1650

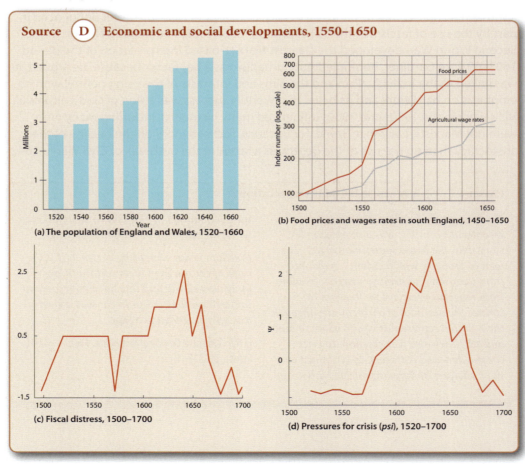

(a) The population of England and Wales, 1520–1660

(b) Food prices and wages rates in south England, 1450–1650

(c) Fiscal distress, 1500–1700

(d) Pressures for crisis (*psi*), 1520–1700

Source (E) **Extracts from the Scottish National Covenant, 1638**

In obedience to the Commandment of God, conform to the practice of the godly in former times, and according to the laudable example of our Worthy and Religious Progenitors, & of many yet living amongst us, which was warranted also by act of Council, commanding a general band to be made and subscribed by his Majesty's subjects, of all ranks, for two causes: One was, For defending the true Religion, as it was then reformed, and is expressed in the Confession of Faith ... We Nobleman, Barons, Gentlemen, Burgesses, Ministers &

Commons under subscribing, considering divers times before & especially at this time, the danger of the true reformed Religion, ... Do hereby profess, and before God, his Angels, and the World solemnly declare. That, with our whole hearts we agree & resolve, all the days of our life, constantly to adhere unto, and to defend the foresaid true Religion ...

The National Covenant, February 1638, quoted in W. C. Dickinson and G. Donaldson (eds) (1961) *A Source Book of Scottish History,* vol. III (1567–1707), Thomas Nelson, pp.100–2.

FOR DISCUSSION

In a small group, consider the following:

To what extent do sources D and E indicate a modification/rejection of 'orthodox' Marxist interpretations of the English Revolution?

Source (F) **How England was divided during the Civil War in 1642**

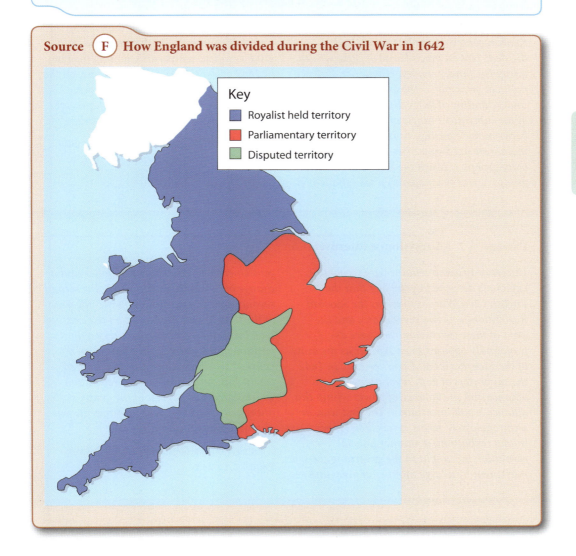

Key
- Royalist held territory
- Parliamentary territory
- Disputed territory

In explaining the Civil War, which *two* approaches are supported by source F?

How does the view taken in passage 5 conflict with passage 4 and sources D and E?

LINK UP

'From above' interpretations – see Chapter 1, page 17.

Local/regional approach – see Chapter 2, page 35.

1. What kind of approach is shown by Professor Everitt in passage 6? What does it contribute to our understanding?

2. Which approach is being criticised in passage 7?

Passage 5 Criticism of economic and social explanations of the Civil War

*Little emerges from such a survey of the economic and social characteristics of seventeenth-century England to lead one to conclude that political upheaval stemmed from socio-economic change. Indeed, paradoxically, continuities may have been at least as important as change. The failure of the economy to grow as fast as did the population meant there were dangerously large numbers in 1642 ready to seek their fortunes in arms. Similarly, the prominence of **primogeniture**, with its attendant problem of the younger brother, undoubtedly helped both king and parliament find their enthusiastic supporters. Had economy and society been better matched there might have been fewer extremists seeking to rise by means of total victory. But in no way does the social structure appear fundamentally unstable ... Nevertheless, on the whole the causes of the war have to be sought in the realm of politics and religion, and in the domain of folly and misunderstanding.*

D. Hirst (1990) *Authority and Conflict: England 1603–1658*, Edward Arnold, pp. 24–5.

Another important development has been a move away from 'top-down' models in explaining the Civil War – instead, historians such as Alan Everitt and others have spearheaded the examination of local conditions as being the main determinants of how the local gentry and aristocracy responded to national issues.

Passage 6 Allegiance of the Kentish gentry during the Civil War

What, then, were the lines upon which the Kentish gentry, in the last resort, had divided? Not on precise lines of class, wealth, antiquity, family rivalry, religion or abstract political principle ... The essential clue to the understanding of party division in Kent, and of the subsequent tangle of relationships between these parties, consists in the fact that there were not two parties in the county, but three groups ... Much the largest of the three groups ... was the moderates, who shaded off into mild 'parliamentarians' supporting the County Committee, on the one hand, and mild 'royalists' temporarily joining the king in 1642 or waiting hopefully at home, on the other. On either wing of this group were two small groups, hardly more than cliques, of genuine Cavaliers and Parliamentarians.

A. Everitt (1966) *The Community of Kent and the Great Rebellion*, Leicester University Press, pp. 116–7.

Passage 7 A revisionist interpretation

Uncertainty about what we are trying to explain is deepened by the fact that the English Civil War, as much as the Russian Revolution, was two revolutions, and the aims of these two revolutions were as profoundly opposed to each other as the aims of the Mensheviks and Bolsheviks ... In 1642 the supporters of both revolutions were in alliance and the balance of power within this alliance is still uncertain ... The first was, in anthropologists' terms, a rebellion rather than a revolution; it was not a social revolution but a split in the governing class; a movement by a large number of peers and gentlemen to force a change of policy and a change of ministers on Charles I. The second revolution was a revolution in the full sense of the term: it was an assault on the existing social structure, and particularly on the position of the gentry ... We have then a political rebellion which was to a limited extent successful, and a social revolution which, largely as a result of the gentry's unbroken control of local government, was almost totally unsuccessful.

C. Russell (1991) *The Origins of the English Civil War*, Macmillan, pp. 2–3.

However, a more far-ranging attack on the Marxist approach came with Robert Ashton's *The English Civil War – Conservatism and Revolution* (1997). Though accepting that there were long-term influences and problems long before 1640, his argument is that Charles I was the 'progressive' in wanting to bring about changes, while the gentry opposing him were 'conservatives' wanting to maintain the traditional constitutional set-up. More fundamental revisions from the pens of Conrad Russell and particularly Kevin Sharpe, argue against long-term causes, and instead claim that there were no real problems until 1637. The English Civil War was forced on unwilling men by the pressure of events.

Passage **8** **Elton's impact on debates concerning the English Revolution**

Finally, among this catalogue of historiographical factors, the work and influence (the mission, one might say) of Geoffrey Elton has also had its bearing on the construction of the seventeenth-century field. [He] has occasionally been known to participate directly in the discussion of Christopher Hill's own work … However, the expenditure of such an enormous career-long effort on establishing the founding importance of a Tudor 'revolution in government' for the course of British history … derives much of its point from an implicit hostility to the Marxist-cum-sociological conception of the English Revolution. It is not too fanciful to regard Hill and Stone (and the ghost of Tawney) as the hidden addressees of Elton's history: hard-headed administrative consolidation became the foundation stone of modern British history, and not the political and ideological consequences of condensed social change, the clash of organised social forces and the struggle to constitute a new moral order; …

G. Eley and W. Hunt (eds) (1988) *Reviving the English Revolution*, Verso Books, p. 3.

Passage **9** **The problems of multiple monarchy**

We have not found the causes of the English Civil War because the question involves trying to discover the whole of the explanation by examining a part of the problem. The English Civil War is regularly discussed as if it were a unique event, but it was not: between 1639 and 1642, Charles I faced armed resistance in all three of his kingdoms … the tendency of dissidents in each kingdom to try to make common cause with sympathisers in the others ensured that the English, Scottish and Irish troubles could not remain three isolated problems: they triggered off a period of repeated intervention by the three kingdoms in each others affairs … We now know, thanks to a large body of work, that the relations between multiple kingdoms were among the main causes of instability in continental Europe, and Professors Elliot and Koenigsberger have been asking for some time whether the rule which applies across the Channel also applies in Britain. This lecture will suggest that the answer to their question is 'yes'.

C. Russell, 'The British Problem and the English Civil War', professorial inaugural lecture, University College London, 1984

Is Elton's approach, as summed up in passage 8, that of an empiricist or a structuralist? Explain your reasoning.

LINK UP

Empirical approaches – see Chapter 1, page 7.

Structural inrpretations – see Chapter 1, page 12.

THINK LIKE AN HISTORIAN

Re-read the case study about the mid-seventeenth-century crisis during the period 1629–42, and work through the two questions that follow:

(a) What can you learn from passage 4 about the interpretations, approaches and methods of this historian? Refer to the extract and your knowledge to explain your answer.

THINK LIKE AN HISTORIAN *continued*

EXAM TIP

When answering question (a), you will need to do *two* things:

(i) Support your answer by *detailed* reference to the extract AND refer to alternative approaches/methods.

(ii) Use relevant and accurate knowledge as part of a thorough analysis of the interpretation.

(b) Some historians, such as Alan Everitt, have focused on local developments in England in the first half of the seventeenth century to explain the causes of the English Civil War in 1642. Explain how this has contributed to our understanding of the mid-seventeenth-century crisis. Has this approach any disadvantages or shortcomings?

EXAM TIP

As with (a) questions, you will have to do *two* things to achieve a top grade in (b) questions:

(i) Show both advantages and disadvantages/shortcomings of the approach/method, AND compare it with other approaches/methods.

(ii) Use relevant and accurate knowledge to assess both advantages and disadvantages.

EXAM TIP

Before submitting your answers and moving on to the next case study, check the key areas checklist on page 51 to make sure you have taken the right approach for a top grade.

Britain's seventeenth-century crises: other aspects of controversy

Apart from the debates surrounding the causes and nature of the Civil War, other aspects of controversy include:

- The nature of Charles I's 11-year personal rule – was it simply effective government, or a tyranny?

- The various explanations relating to the reasons for Parliament's victory in the Civil War, and for the execution of the king.

- The nature, impact and significance of the constitutional, political, religious and economic developments during the Commonwealth and Republican periods.

- The impact of the Civil War and Interregnum on the restored monarchy, and on longer-term social and economic developments.

- Whether Britain was closer to absolutism after 1660, and the nature and importance of the 'Glorious Revolution' of 1688–9.

Stretch and challenge

Consider this summary of historical approaches: Marxist interpretations of the Civil War and its origins looked for the inevitable rise of the bourgeoisie. Whig interpretations were no different, except that the inevitable progress they worked to identify was the rise of Parliament.

1. What does it tell us about the approach taken by many historians?

2. What have the questions of the revisionists added to the arguments over the causes of the Civil War?

3. Do historians tend to create more problems than they solve?

Case study 3: Different interpretations of British Imperialism, c.1850–c.1950

Introduction

The history of the British **empire** and British **imperialism** is far-reaching: covering not just the directly or indirectly ruled British colonies, but also those regions which, though nominally independent, were under the economic sway of British imperialism – often referred to as Britain's 'informal' empire.

The history of British imperialism also encompasses:

- the nature and impact of British imperial authority and rule
- British attitudes to race, religion and nationalism
- the impact and legacy of empire – economically and socially – on people in Britain itself.

The following extracts focus on the 'New Imperialism' period of 1870–1914, which saw considerable imperial expansion. This is itself part of the period 1815–1914, seen by many historians as Britain's 'imperial century'. However, these periods involve all the main historical arguments which relate to British imperialism in general during the period 1850–1950, in particular, those concerning the relative importance of Britain's expanding industrial economy to what is known as the partition of Africa (see source A).

Broadly speaking, there are three main historical interpretations of, or approaches to, the study and explanation of British imperialism:

- Those that focus on developments within Britain – *metropolitan approaches*.
- Those that focus on factors within the colonies and territories themselves – *peripheral approaches*.
- Those that seek explanations in developments on the wider European or world/ global scene – *international relations approaches*.

Until the 1950s, historians tended to accept that there was a period of 'indifference' to empire in Britain in the first half of the nineteenth century. Instead, the focus was said to be on free trade, with doubts about the value of empire which, in the eighteenth century, had been seen as providing supplies of raw materials and markets for goods. However, when trying to explain the significant expansion of the British empire after the 1850s – mainly in Africa and Asia – the early historical approaches tended to focus on developments in Britain, especially on the links between industrial expansion in

Empire

An empire consists of a collection of different subordinate (peripheral) states, areas and peoples, scattered around the world and controlled by one strong ruling (metropolitan) state, such as the Roman Empire or the British Empire. The nature of rule can vary, i.e. direct, through local 'clients', or via economic controls.

Imperialism

Imperialism is the reasons for and processes of establishing and maintaining an empire. However, there are various approaches for analysing these reasons/processes. The three main ones include:

- a metropolitan/'top down' approach
- a peripheral approach
- an international relations/'world-view' approach.

Britain (the metropole) and, in particular, on the growing need for guaranteed raw materials and markets, and the export of surplus capital.

The first main metropolitan explanation was put forward in 1902 by J. A. Hobson, in his *Imperialism: A Study*. He argued that an unequal distribution of wealth in Britain resulted in a surplus of capital, which it was more profitable to export to and invest in undeveloped overseas outlets. This view is shown in the extract from his study given in passage 1.

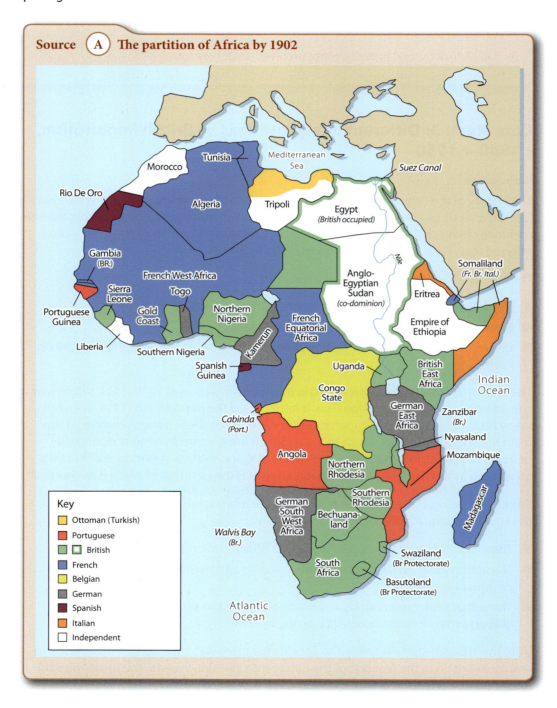

Source **A** The partition of Africa by 1902

Key

- Ottoman (Turkish)
- Portuguese
- British
- French
- Belgian
- German
- Spanish
- Italian
- Independent

Passage ① 'The taproot of imperialism'

It is this economic condition of affairs that forms the taproot of imperialism. If the consuming public in this country raised its standard of consumption to keep pace with every rise of productive powers, there could be no excess of goods or capital clamorous to use imperialism in order to find markets.

It is not industrial progress that demands the opening up of new markets and areas of investment, but mal-distribution of consuming power which prevents the absorption of commodities and capital within the country.

J. A. Hobson (1902) *Imperialism: A Study.*

A similar metropolitan explanation of imperialism, also based on economics, was developed by Lenin in his *Imperialism: The Highest Stage of Capitalism*, published in 1916. Lenin's Marxist interpretation saw imperial expansion in the late nineteenth century as a capitalist crisis and conflict over markets, which had been a major factor in the outbreak of the First World War. A more modern and nuanced Marxist historical interpretation of British (and European) imperialism is shown in passage 2.

Passage ② A Marxist interpretation of British imperialism

The era of the Great Depression also initiated the era of imperialism; the formal imperialism of the 'partition of Africa' in the 1880s, the semi-formal imperialism of national or international consortia taking over the financial management of weak countries, the informal imperialism of foreign investment. Political historians have professed to find no economic reasons for this virtual division of the world between a handful of West European powers (plus the USA) in the last decades of the nineteenth century. Economic historians have had no

such difficulty. Imperialism was not a new thing for Britain. What was new was the end of the virtual British monopoly in the undeveloped world, and the consequent necessity to mark out regions of imperial influence formally against potential competitors; often ahead of any actual prospects of economic benefits, often, it must be admitted, with disappointing economic results.

E. J. Hobsbawm (1971) *Industry and Empire*, Pelican/ Penguin, p.131.

These metropolitan economic-based interpretations of imperialism have been criticised by studies which point out how relatively little capital was in fact invested in the African and Asian territories acquired between 1870 and 1914, compared with investments in the 'informal' empire of Latin America (see source E although passage 2 also refers to this aspect). However, approaches which emphasise that imperialism was the result of metropolitan economic developments have recently been given some partial support by P. J. Cain and A. G. Hopkins, in their study, *British Imperialism: Innovation and Expansion 1688–1914* (1993). Although this rejects the Marxist interpretations which emphasise the links between industrialisation and imperial expansion, they stress the importance of finance capital (especially the City of London) and the emergence of a new 'Gentlemanly Capitalist' elite. One of their conclusions is that 'Explanations of imperialism ought to begin with a close study of economic structure and change in Britain'. This view, in turn, has been criticised by others, such as A. Porter, for ignoring other influences in British imperial expansion, while D. Cannadine and D. K. Fieldhouse do not see such a hard divide between the industrial and finance-service sectors in the British economy.

In opposition to metropolitan explanations is the peripheral approach, which places more emphasis on developments and changes in the undeveloped territories which were at the receiving end of imperialism, and how these interacted with European

Passage 1 is an example of which type of historical approach?

LINK UP

Marxist interpretations – see Chapter 1, page 13.

What aspects of passage 2 suggest that the historian is putting forward a Marxist interpretation for the partition of Africa?

desires. For instance, J. Gallagher and R. Robinson pioneered this approach in their article, 'The imperialism of free trade' (1953) and later their book, *Africa and the Victorians: The Official Mind of Imperialism* (1961). Their revisionist argument claims that Britain had always followed a consistent policy, based on free trade and a preference for 'informal' control, rather than formal or direct rule, and rejects arguments that imperial expansion was primarily the result of industrial or financial developments in Britain. It was only when local developments – including the emergence of nationalist movements – or potential disorder (or the actions of a rival power in the area) threatened trade that imperial expansion took place (see source B). In particular, they argue that a combination of rising nationalism, weakness of the Egyptian ruler and French interests, which threatened Britain's strategic and trade interests, led to the partition of Africa (see source D).

Can source B be used to support a 'peripheral' or 'metropolitan' interpretation of late nineteenth-century imperialism? Quote extracts to justify your choice.

Source B — A request for British rule from the kings of the Cameroons River, West Africa, 1881

Dear Mr. Gladstone,

We both your servants have met this afternoon to write you these few lines of writing trusting it may find you in a good state of health as it leaves us at present. As we heard you are the chief man in the House of Commons, so we may write to tell you that we want to be under Her Majesty's control. We want our country to be governed by the *British government. We are tired of governing this country ourselves, every dispute leads to war, and often great loss of lives, so we think it is best thing to give up the country to you British men with no doubt it will bring peace, civilisation and Christianity in the country.*

King Bell and King Acqua of the Cameroons River, West Africa, 6 November 1881.

Another version of the peripheral approach is the focus on the role played by 'men on the spot' in encouraging their respective governments to become involved or to take certain actions. It is claimed that some of these men had grand schemes of their own, often working with local rulers to achieve their ends. Alternatively, local officials sometimes made decisions which were not requested by the British government, but which led to developments that eventually required government intervention. An example of the 'man on the spot' factor is given in source C, with **Cecil Rhodes** playing a huge part in British imperial expansion in southern Africa.

BIOGRAPHY

Cecil Rhodes (1853–1902) was born in Britain. He arrived in South Africa in 1870 and quickly made a fortune out of diamond mining. He eventually became Prime Minister of Cape Colony and ruthlessly expanded British rule in the region.

Source C — Cecil Rhodes – 'man on the spot'

I contend that we are the first race in the world and that the more of the world we inhabit the better it is for the human race. I contend that every acre added to our territory means the birth of more of the English race who otherwise might not be brought into existence. Added to this, the absorption of the greater portion of the world under our rule simply means the end to all *wars ... The furtherance of the British Empire, for bringing the whole of the uncivilised world under British rule, for the recovery of the United States, for making the Anglo-Saxon race but one Empire. What a dream! but yet it is possible. It is possible!*

Cecil Rhodes, quoted in F. McDonough (1994) *The British Empire, 1815–1914*, Hodder Murray, pp. 33–4.

FOR DISCUSSION

In a small group, consider the following:

To what extent does source C provide useful evidence for a 'man on the spot' explanation of British imperialism?

A third major approach to imperialism focuses on international relations. In such interpretations, historians such as A. J. P. Taylor emphasise pressures and considerations which include the perceived need to protect existing colonies or influence from other rival states. Some, such as G. N. Sanderson, see French expansion as pre-dating the British occupation of Egypt in 1882. Others see the Berlin Conference of 1884–5 as being the main cause of the partition of Africa. However, some historians such as D. K. Fieldhouse now place more importance on developments within Africa itself. On the other hand, P. Kennedy (who combines evidence from metropolitan and peripheral approaches) sees the partition of Africa as being the result of other European states trying to follow Britain's lead, and Britain then responding in order to protect its imperial dominance.

Source D The importance of the Suez Canal to British trade

Egypt forms our highway to India and the East generally ... As regards the Suez Canal, England has a double interest; it has a predominant commercial interest, because 82% of the trade passing through the Canal is British trade, and it has a predominant political interest caused by the fact that the Canal is the principal highway to India, Ceylon, the Straits and British Burmah, where 250,000,000 live under our rule; and

also to China where we have vast interests and 84% of the external trade of the still more enormous Empire. It is also one of the roads to our Colonial Empire in Australia and New Zealand.

From a speech by Sir Charles Dilke, Under-Secretary of State for Foreign Affairs, 25 July 1882, in *Hansard's parliamentary debates*, Commons, vol. 272, col. 1720.

> Which broad historical approach(es) could source D be used to support?

Other aspects of imperialism which have been explored are the financial benefits of empire (see passage 2). For instance, L. E. Davis and R. A. Huttenbach claim that higher rates of return were obtained from investments outside the empire, while the empire itself required significant subsidies. However, this view has been criticised by scholars such as A. Offer, especially in relation to India, which he claims subsidised Britain.

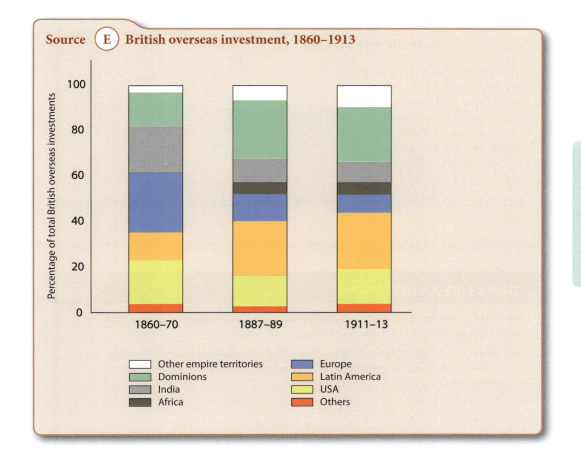

Source E British overseas investment, 1860–1913

Percentage of total British overseas investments

y-axis: 0, 20, 40, 60, 80, 100

x-axis: 1860–70, 1887–89, 1911–13

Legend:
- Other empire territories
- Dominions
- India
- Africa
- Europe
- Latin America
- USA
- Others

> In understanding the partition of Africa, how might source E be used to point out some of the weaknesses of (a) a Marxist approach, and (b) a metropolitan/economic explanation?

Finally, historians have examined the social, psychological and cultural impacts of empire on Britain itself. As sources F and G suggest, arrogance and racism towards other ethnic groups were negative effects of considerable significance, especially from the 1890s.

1. How would a nationalist historian use source F?

2. What does source F tell us about the impact of the empire on Britain by the mid-1870s?

3. How are sources F and G useful to historical explanations that focus on the impact of imperialism in Britain?

Source (F) **Disraeli makes Queen Victoria Empress of India, 1876**

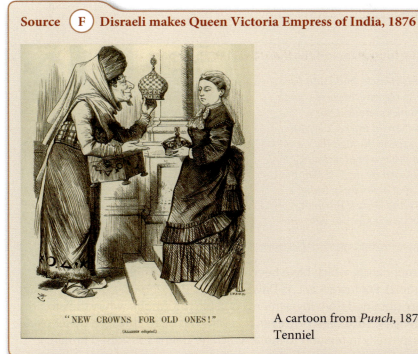

"NEW CROWNS FOR OLD ONES!"

(Aladdin adapted.)

A cartoon from *Punch*, 1876, drawn by John Tenniel

Source (G) **'The White Man's Burden'**

Take up the White Man's Burden –
Send forth the best ye breed –
Go bind your sons to exile
To serve your captives' need;
To wait in heavy harness
On fluttered folk and wild –
Your new-caught, sullen peoples
Half-devil and half-child.

From R. Kipling's 'The White Man's Burden', written in 1899. Kipling wrote this poem to encourage the USA to build an empire.

THINK LIKE AN HISTORIAN

Re-read the case study about British imperialism in the late nineteenth century, and work through the two questions that follow:

(a) What can you learn from passage 2 about the interpretations, approaches and methods of this historian? Refer to the extract and your knowledge to explain your answer.

THINK LIKE AN HISTORIAN continued

EXAM TIP

When answering question (a), you will need to do *two* things:

(i)   Support your answer by *detailed* reference to the extract AND refer to alternative approaches/methods.

(ii) Use relevant and accurate knowledge as part of a thorough analysis of the interpretation.

(b) Some historians have focused on the significance of 'the men on the spot' to explain the 'New Imperialism' of the late nineteenth century. Explain how this has contributed to our understanding of British imperialism. Has this approach any disadvantages or shortcomings?

EXAM TIP

As with (a) questions, you will have to do *two* things to achieve a top grade in (b) questions:

(i)   Show both advantages and disadvantages/shortcomings of the approach/method, AND compare it with other approaches/methods.

(ii) Use relevant and accurate knowledge to assess both advantages and disadvantages.

EXAM TIP

Before submitting your answer and moving on to the next case study, check the checklist on page 51 to make sure you have taken the right approach for a top grade.

British imperialism: other aspects of controversy

Apart from the debates concerning a 'New imperialism', other aspects of controversy include:

- The initial nature of mid-nineteenth century imperialism, and whether there was an 'anti-imperialism' period.
- The relative importance of metropolitan, peripheral and international relations factors in the development of the British Empire.
- The role and significance of women in the development of the British Empire.
- The impact of Empire in the colonial countries and on Britain.
- The reasons and developments which led to the loss of Empire, including the relative importance of factors such as war and anti-colonial movements.

Stretch and challenge

Consider how concepts of race have changed over time.

How did this affect the ways in which empire was seen in the late nineteenth century?

How has this affected ways of seeing empire since?

Case study 4: The debate over British appeasement in the 1930s

Introduction

LINK UP

Intentionalist interpretations – see Chapter 1, page 11.

Structural interpretations – see Chapter 1, page 12.

Appeasement

This refers to the foreign policy which British (and French) governments adopted to deal with the implications of a possible aggressor. At first, it was used to keep reasonable relations with Mussolini. Later it was applied to Hitler's foreign policy during the 1930s.

EXAM TIP

When starting to investigate different historical interpretations and explanations of British appeasement, make sure you go beyond a 'labels/schools of thought' approach. Instead, try to examine closely the evidence historians have used, and the strengths/weaknesses of their explanations.

As well as the on-going historical debate about Hitler's role in the outbreak of the Second World War (between the orthodox Hitlocentric/'intentionalist' and the structuralist/'revisionist' historians), there is considerable debate about the role of Neville Chamberlain and the purpose of the British policy of **appeasement** in the 1930s.

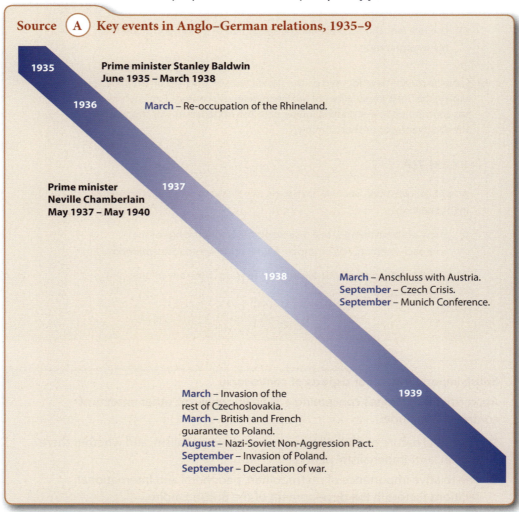

Source (**A**) **Key events in Anglo–German relations, 1935–9**

1935 — **Prime minister Stanley Baldwin June 1935 – March 1938**

1936 — **March** – Re-occupation of the Rhineland.

Prime minister Neville Chamberlain May 1937 – May 1940 — **1937**

1938 — **March** – Anschluss with Austria.
September – Czech Crisis.
September – Munich Conference.

1939 — **March** – Invasion of the rest of Czechoslovakia.
March – British and French guarantee to Poland.
August – Nazi-Soviet Non-Aggression Pact.
September – Invasion of Poland.
September – Declaration of war.

The early historical views of Chamberlain as, at best, an incompetent leader, and appeasement as a morally bankrupt policy have been revised in several ways since 1945. At the other extreme, for instance, some revisionist historians see Chamberlain as an able politician with a clear grasp of Britain's economic and military strengths; of the issue of reliable allies (see sources C and D) and of Hitler's deceptions; and who therefore tried to maintain peace while also preparing for war.

The following extracts focus on British foreign policy in the late 1930s, but involve considering the main historical interpretations about the policy of appeasement throughout the 1930s, which had to deal with the expansion of Nazi Germany as shown in source B.

Even before the end of the Second World War, initial judgements of Chamberlain and the policy of appeasement were extremely critical. The earliest classic or 'orthodox' condemnation of appeasement was offered as early as 1940 by 'Cato' (a collective pseudonym for several leftwing critics of appeasement) in their *Guilty Men* booklet. It condemned Chamberlain as a 'guilty man', and portrayed appeasement as a shameful combination of deliberate deception of British public opinion, incompetent leadership and diplomacy, and extremely poor military planning.

Source **B** **Nazi Germany's expansion, 1933–9**

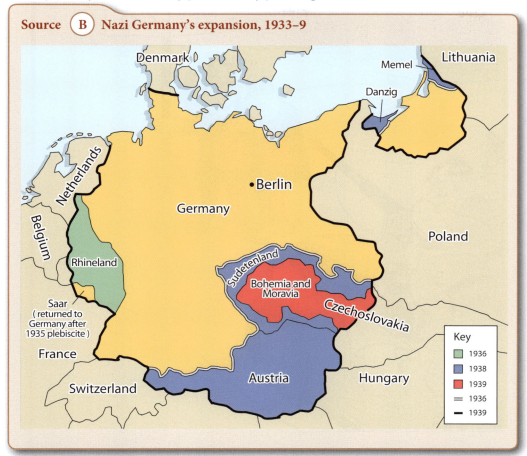

One of the first post-war historical studies of appeasement appeared in 1948, when J. Wheeler-Bennett judged Chamberlain as a leader whose appeasement policy and diplomacy was both morally wrong and politically ineffective. Then, in the 1950s and 1960s, several memoirs from contemporary politicians, diplomats and officials – such as Winston Churchill and Anthony Eden – seemed to support this view.

However, from 1967, the 30-year rule allowed historians access to government documents relating to the late 1930s. There soon appeared a series of history books and articles 'revising' the previous 'orthodox' view. These revisionist historians (such as D. Dilks, M. Cowling and J. Charmley) see Chamberlain's policy of appeasement as a realistic way of dealing with the structural difficulties faced by Britain in the late 1930s. Chamberlain, instead of being a 'guilty man', was portrayed as making sound and logical judgements, based on Britain and France's initial inability in the period 1937 to early 1939 to fight a war in Europe with any realistic chance of success.

Source **C** **An extract from Chamberlain's diary entry, 26 March 1939**

I must confess to a most profound distrust of Russia. I have no belief whatever in her ability to maintain an effective offensive, even if she wanted to. And I distrust her motives which seem to me to have little connection with our ideas of liberty, and to *be concerned only with getting everyone by the ears. Moreover, she is both hated and suspected by the smaller states, notably, Poland, Rumania and Finland.*

Quoted in K. Feiling (1946) *The Life of Neville Chamberlain*, Macmillan, p. 403.

Explain how a Marxist historian might use source D as part of their explanation of British foreign policy in the period 1938–9?

LINK UP

Marxist interpretations – see Chapter 1, page 13.

Source **D** **A view from the Soviet Union on Britain's betrayal of Czechoslovakia in 1938 at Munich**

Such structural factors included Britain's economic problems, its short-term military weaknesses (facing Japanese aggression in the Far East as well as the European dictators) and the strength of public opinion against significant rearmament. These revisionist assessments of British appeasement as a clear-sighted response to foreign affairs in the second half of the 1930s are illustrated by sources E, F and G. In fact, both Cowley and Charmley even argued that appeasement should have been continued after March 1939, in view of Britain's economic and military weaknesses.

Source **E** **'The Peace Ballot,' 1934**

Question 2: Are you in favour of an all-round reduction of armaments by international agreement?

Yes: 10,058,026 *votes*

No: 815,365 *votes*

Votes in favour as a percentage of all answers (Yes, No, Doubtful, Abstentions): 90.7

League of Nations Union, 1935.

Source F Military strength of the European powers, 1938–9

Army strength (fully equipped army divisions)

Country	January 1938	August 1939
Germany	81	130
Great Britain	2	4
France	63	86
Italy	73	73
Soviet Union	125	125
Czechoslovakia	34	0
Poland	500	500

Airforce strength (number of available aircraft)

Country	January 1938	August 1939
Germany	1820	4210
Great Britain	1050	1750
France	1195	1234
Italy	1301	1531
Soviet Union	3050	3361
Czechoslovakia	600	0
Poland	500	500

A. Adamthwaite (1977) *The Making of the Second World War*, Allen & Unwin, p. 227.

Source G 'Appreciation of the Situation in the Event of War against Germany', 1938

It is our opinion that no pressure that Great Britain and France can bring to bear, either by sea, on land, or in the air, could prevent Germany from overrunning Bohemia and from inflicting a decisive defeat on Czechoslovakia. The restoration of Czechoslovakia's lost integrity could only be achieved by the defeat of Germany and as the outcome of a prolonged struggle, which from the outset must assume the character of an unlimited war.

The intervention of Italy and/or Japan on the side of Germany would create a situation which the Chiefs of Staff in the Mediterranean and Middle East Appreciation described in the following language: 'Moreover, war against Japan, Germany and Italy simultaneously in 1938 is a commitment which neither the present nor the projected strength of our defence forces is designed to meet, even if we were in alliance with France and Russia, and which would, therefore, place a dangerous strain on the resources of the Empire ...'.

From Chiefs of Staff Report: 'Appreciation of the Situation in the Event of War against Germany', 14 September 1938.

> Explain how sources E, F and G contribute to a structuralist/revisionist explanation of British appeasement?

However, one of the main weaknesses of these revisionist interpretations is their strong reliance on the official documents of British governments and leading ministers, as these were drafted, collected and selected by those who supported appeasement. With the exception of Cowling, revisionist interpretations have tended to ignore the existence of alternative policies and, in particular, to have overlooked the intelligence reports which Chamberlain and the Foreign Office received relating to Hitler's intentions to dominate Europe by the use of military means.

Consequently, there followed a counter to the revisionist approach to appeasement. Some of the historians involved, including K. Middlemas and R. A. C. Parker, have criticised Chamberlain for pushing through and then sticking to a policy which was misguided, and for deliberately misleading public opinion. Parker, in particular, stresses the quick rejection of alternative policies; while other – often Marxist – historians have stressed the ingrained hostility to communism of an elite political class, which resulted in a refusal until too late to consider seriously the concept of a 'Grand Alliance' with the USSR against Nazi threats, as even Churchill suggested. Adamthwaite's extract in passage 1 is an example of such an approach.

> **Passage** **A counter to the revisionist approach**
>
> *It has become almost axiomatic in assessments of British and French leaders to see them as realistic statesmen, oppressed by the knowledge of their countries' weaknesses and the strengths of potential enemies. The uncritical premise of these assessments is that the policy pursued was the only practicable one at the time. In fact there were many variables, and ministerial appraisals were the product of prejudice and opinion …*
>
> *The feebleness and timidity of British and French foreign policies in the late 1930s were symptomatic of the shortsighted selfishness of a ruling class set on self-preservation.*
>
> A. Adamthwaite (1977), p. 95.

What are the strengths and weaknesses of the approach indicated in passage 1?

The newer approach, however, takes on aspects of the revisionist explanations of appeasement, in particular, some of the real structural constraints and problems facing British governments. It offers an, arguably, more balanced interpretation, such as suggested by passages 2 and 3.

> **Passage** **Dilks' views on appeasement**
>
> *In other words, the buying of time remained a strong element in British foreign policy, as it had been for several years. This was the line which Eden had recommended to the Cabinet early in 1936; to reach agreements with Germany where they could honourably be reached, to be under no illusions that Germany would keep them when they ceased to suit her, and to accelerate British rearmament, the spending upon which was moving swiftly forward in 1938 and 1939 and which far exceeded any expenditure upon arms ever undertaken by Britain in peace time. This is not to say that the sole purpose of the policy pursued in 1938 was simply to obtain a breathing space. Chamberlain had some sympathy for German grievances, and was acutely sensible of Hitler's capacity to exploit them; he felt much doubt about the outcome of a war; he could hardly bear to think of the wanton destruction; but there is not a sign he felt any fondness for dictatorships or sneaking sympathy for fascism.*
>
> D. Dilks, in Lord Butler (ed.) (1977) *The Conservatives: A History of their Origins to 1965*, Allen & Unwin.

What kind of approach/ explanation is being taken by the writer of passage 2?

Such post-revisionist interpretations, for instance, suggest that when the international circumstances changed concerning the possibility of allies, Chamberlain dropped appeasement (see passage 4). However, it has been argued that the delay in declaring war after Nazi Germany's invasion of Poland shows that Neville Chamberlain had not fully abandoned appeasement even then, and was possibly looking for a Polish 'Munich' in order to keep Britain out of a new war.

Passage 3   A more recent interpretation

A very important element in interwar diplomacy was fear of the spread of Communism. Bolshevik propaganda, aimed at subverting capitalist governments and inciting workers' revolution, alarmed governments throughout Europe ...

By the late 1930s, it was becoming clear that German eastward expansion could be checked only by concerted action on the part of British and French leaders, working together with Stalin. However, two decades of ideological warfare had created profound suspicions between the Western government and Soviet Russia. Neither side trusted the other. On what basis could an agreement be reached?

Russian troops could get to Germany only by crossing Polish territory. This the Polish government violently opposed, fearing that once the troops were on Polish soil they would never leave. British and French leaders were not in any position to force the Poles to change their minds, even if they had wished to. It is hardly surprising that Stalin felt the British and French leaders were not serious in their attempts to stop Nazi expansion. After all, Russia had not been invited to the discussions involving the **Sudeten Germans** at Munich.

R. Henig, 'Appeasement and the Origins of the Second World War', in *Perspectives*.

Passage 4   Changes in British circumstances and attitudes in 1939

Throughout 1939 Hitler entirely misread western intentions. After Munich, Britain and France rallied at last to the armed defence of the status quo. Both states speeded up military preparations, until by the summer their combined aircraft and tank production exceeded Germany's. There developed a popular nationalist revival which turned public opinion in both states strongly against Germany and in favour of firmer action. In the summer of 1939, 87% of Britons and 76% of Frenchmen, subjects of earlier opinion polling, recorded a firm commitment to fight if Germany invaded Poland and seized Danzig. Hitlerism was now regarded as a profound threat to the survival of western values and interests, and

Poland was chosen as an issue not for its own sake, but to demonstrate to Hitler the west's determination to defend those interests when threatened. Their empires rallied to the cause too. Canada abandoned neutrality; Australia and New Zealand pledged support; colonial armies were raised in French North Africa, India and Indo-China. Even neutral America began to give encouragement to the western cause, though Roosevelt was too wary of isolationist opinion to commit the United States to a more active or military policy.

R. Overy (1994) *The Inter-War Crisis, 1919–1939*, Longman, p. 89.

THINK LIKE AN HISTORIAN

Re-read the case study about British appeasement in the late 1930s, and work through the two questions that follow:

(a) What can you learn from passage 1 about the interpretations, approaches and methods of this historian? Refer to the extract and your knowledge to explain your answer.

QUICK FACT

The Sudetenland, a region of Czechoslovakia bordering Austria and Germany, contained 3 million German-speakers (**Sudeten Germans**) and, before the peace treaties of 1919–20, had previously been part of Austria. It contained Czechoslovakia's main defences, and the important Skoda armaments and truck works.

FOR DISCUSSION

In a small group, consider the following:

How has Ruth Henig in passage 3 changed the way in which appeasement is viewed?

Read passage 4 in conjunction with sources E, F and G. To what extent do the three latter sources support the historical interpretation suggested in passage 4? Write down the key similarities and differences.

THINK LIKE AN HISTORIAN *continued*

EXAM TIP

When answering question (a), you will need to do *two* things:

(i)   Support your answer by *detailed* reference to the extract AND refer to alternative approaches/methods.

(ii) Use relevant and accurate knowledge as part of a thorough analysis of the interpretation.

(b) Some historians have focused on aspects of human agency to explain the British government's actions in the late 1930s. Explain how this has contributed to our understanding of British appeasement. Has this approach any disadvantages or shortcomings?

EXAM TIP

When answering question (a), you will need to do *two* things:

As with (a) questions, you will have to do *two* things to achieve a top grade in (b) questions:

(i)   Show both advantages and disadvantages/shortcomings of the approach/method, AND compare it with other approaches/methods.

(ii) Use relevant and accurate knowledge to assess both advantages <u>and</u> disadvantages.

EXAM TIP

Before submitting your answer to the questions above and moving on to the next case study, check the key areas checklist on page 51 to make sure you have taken the right approach for a top grade.

The debate over British appeasement in the 1930s: other aspects of controversy

Apart from the debates relating to the nature of British foreign policy in the late 1930s, other aspects of controversy include:

- Hitler and Nazi foreign policy – how far was Hitler in control? Did he have a clear plan and did he follow it?

- The various factors influencing the attitudes of British people to Hitler and Nazi foreign policy during this period.

- The factors influencing Chamberlain and the British government concerning appeasement. Did the have 'freedom of choice'? Was the policy of appeasement rational, mistaken or 'immoral'?

Stretch and challenge

'Chamberlain remains "guilty" in a sense that attached to few other figures in British history.' (D. J. Dutton (2006) *Cato's Guilty Men*, Oxford Dictionary of National Biography)

1. Trace the ways in which Cato's 'Guilty Men' concept influenced subsequent understanding of appeasement.

2. By what methods did historians finally break Cato's view?

3. Can Chamberlain ever recover from Cato's character assassination and be viewed (as in 1938) as a great British leader?

Exam Café
Relax, refresh, result!

Relax and prepare

What I wish I had known at the start of the year …

Laura

I wish I'd followed my teacher's advice from the beginning of the course about the need to carry out regular reading and note-making – something I hadn't really done at AS! Before I knew it, the supervised task was just around the corner – my class notes were so limited, I began the task knowing my result would be disappointing.

Ali

It took me too long to develop a critical AND balanced approach to the various historical methods, approaches and interpretations in the (b) questions. I tended to allow my particular preferences to stop me from properly considering their weaknesses, and from seeing the strengths in opposing approaches. Now that I'm more objective, my marks HAVE improved!

Rosie

At first, I tended to ignore the extracts given in (a) questions, but now I know I need to make specific references to them to get the top grades. I also didn't appreciate in (b) questions that it just wasn't enough to attach labels to historians, or to identify different historical approaches. It took me some time to grasp the need to EXPLAIN the strengths and weaknesses of the different interpretations, approaches and methods, and the evidence they used – and to include DETAILED pieces of own knowledge as part of my assessment.

Getting started…

What's so different about A2?

▷ Although it builds on work done for AS History, it's harder. Even if you did well, you'll have to do more reading and thinking for A2 – in particular, you'll need to keep up to date with your research and note-making so that you'll be ready for the supervised task (see below).

▷ The AS consisted of two written exam papers. The A2 approach is different. The Historical Controversies units will be assessed through a supervised task, in which you'll be asked two questions on your chosen period. It's likely that you'll do the task during normal lesson time over a two-week period.

▷ The supervised task isn't a memory test, as you'll be able to bring your notes and books in with you. This means you'll need good notes/comments to help you fully assess the various extracts and interpretations relating to your chosen topic.

▷ The main skills you'll need are the ability to show what an extract tells you about the interpretation/approach/method of an historian; and the ability to explain how a particular approach has contributed to an understanding of a topic.

Refresh your memory

Different interpretations of British Imperialism, c. 1850–c. 1950 checklist:

▷ *British imperialism in 1850.*
You should know something of the preceding aspects of Britain's empire, in particular: arguments about continuity, the 'imperialism' of free trade, whether there was an 'indifference'/'hostility' to empire by the mid-nineteenth century, the idea of an 'informal' empire, and the various influences on British imperial policy.

▷ *Economic developments in Britain, 1850–1914.*
In particular, you will need to know about the Industrial Revolution's later developments, the impact of the 'Great Depression', and increased European/international rivalry over economic and imperial interests. You will also need to be aware of how these issues were linked to developments and events in Africa and Asia, and how they contributed to the partition of Africa and expansion in Asia during this period.

▷ *Different interpretations of British imperialism.*
In particular, the differences – and relative strengths and weaknesses – between metropolitan theories (e.g. Hobson, Lenin, Hobsbawm, Cain and Hopkins) and peripheral approaches (e.g. Gallagher and Robinson, Fieldhouse). You will also need to understand the global or international theories approach (e.g. Taylor, Kennedy).

EXAM TIP

▷ The (a) question in the two-part supervised task always asks you to consider what you can learn from the passage about:

- the interpretation
- the approach
- the method

of the historian quoted.

▷ Don't forget to take your class-notes and books with you on the day!

▷ You may be allowed to access the Internet while doing the task. If so, remember to bring along a note of the most useful websites.

Get the result !

Question

Read the following extract about British imperialism in the period 1870–1914, and then answer the questions which follow.

(a) What can you learn from the extract about the interpretation, approaches and methods of the historian? Refer to the extract and your own knowledge to explain your answer. [30]

(b) When studying the reasons for British imperialism, some historians have focused on social, economic and political factors in the regions colonised by Britain. What are the advantages and disadvantages of this approach? [30]

EXAM TIP

Remember in (a) questions to:

▷ make specific/detailed references to the extract to support your comments on the approach the historian has used in order to arrive at their interpretation

▷ compare this approach to alternative approaches/interpretations

▷ show how the historian's approach has shaped their interpretation, and consider how far that approach influenced their conclusion.

Extract

In India, the formal Empire never ceased to be vital to the British economy. Elsewhere it appeared to become increasingly vital after the 1870s, when foreign competition became acute, and Britain sought to escape from it – and largely did escape from it – by a flight into her dependencies. From the 1880s 'imperialism' – the division of the world into formal colonies and 'spheres of influence' of the great powers, generally combined with the attempt to establish the sort of economic satellite system which Britain had evolved spontaneously – became universally popular among the large powers. For Britain this was a step back. She exchanged the informal empire over most of the underdeveloped world for the formal empire of a quarter of it, plus the older satellite economies.

Nor was the change particularly easy or inviting. The really valuable satellite economies were (except for India) either beyond political control – like the Argentine – or they were white settler 'dominions' with their own economic interests, which did not necessarily coincide with Britain's. They required compensatory concessions for their own products in Britain, if they were to hand over their markets entirely to the mother country, and it was on this point that Joseph Chamberlain's plans for imperial integration broke down in the early 1900s.

There was some point in annexing all the backward areas possible in order to secure control of the raw materials in them, which even at the end of the nineteenth century increasingly looked as though they would be vital for modern economies, and which indeed became vital.

Rosie's answer: question (a)

This extract relates to the late nineteenth century, which some historians have referred to as the 'New Imperialism'. This period is seen by such historians as being a marked change from the 'age of indifference' to empire which is said to have existed during the years 1815–70. This 'traditional'/orthodox view has, however, been criticised by revisionist historians such as Gallagher and Robinson, who have tended to see continuity with an earlier 'informal' empire.

The comment in the first paragraph of the extract about the empire being 'vital to the British economy' suggests that this historian is clearly putting forward a metropolitan interpretation of imperialism. In fact, this historian seems to be taking a Marxist approach to explain British imperial expansion in this period as they appear to be trying to explain this expansion largely as a result of industrial developments and technological advances in Britain. Historians taking such an approach tend to refer to the great industrial expansion which took place in Britain in the years 1815–60, when it was responsible for 60 per cent of the total growth of world manufacturing.

Metropolitan interpretations, which are based on the economic factors in Britain itself, were first put forward by Hobson in 1902, who referred to the importance of surplus finance capital. A specifically Marxist version was published later by Lenin in 1916, claiming that an economic crisis in late nineteenth-century monopoly capitalism led to imperial rivalry between European states competing for raw materials and markets. The last paragraph of the extract in fact refers to this desire to control raw materials which, by the end of the nineteenth century, had become 'vital for modern economies'. This is typical of a metropolitan/Marxist approach. Overall this extract, which includes references to the existence of a formal empire and to rivalry between states, seems to belong clearly to this approach..

Examiner says:

Rosie makes a good start with an introduction which gives an overall view of the historian's extract, including an awareness of several relevant interpretations/approaches.

Examiner says:

Rosie is engaging directly with the extract and she has also shown some knowledge of the particular approach and some specific knowledge of the evidence used by such an approach.

Examiner says:

In paragraphs 2 and 3, Rosie shows clear understanding of the historian's approach and method.

Examiner says:

Again, there are some useful comments on metropolitan interpretations, and knowledge about some of the main theorists of this approach and the arguments they put forward.

However, there are other interpretations of British imperialism in this period — several of which have criticised the explicitly Marxist versions of the metropolitan approach, because of the failure to fully consider other factors. In 1993, Cain and Hopkins put forward their theory of 'Gentlemanly Capitalism' which instead places more emphasis on the financial and service sectors of the British economy — in particular, the City of London in which, after 1870, 'gentlemanly capitalists' invested heavily. London became the international centre for banking and finance, with British capital investments abroad rising from £30 million in 1851 to £70 million in 1871. In fact, though, this can be seen as a partial rehabilitation of Hobson's metropolitan views about surplus capital.

However, there are also revisionist interpretations which specifically reject the metropolitan approach and its focus on developments in Britain — instead, such approaches argue that imperial expansion in the years after 1870 can be better explained by what happened in the 'periphery' (the areas being colonised). This approach was spearheaded by Gallagher and Robinson in the 1950s and early 1960s: in particular, they stressed the importance of local crises leading the British government to take action in the late nineteenth century. For instance, the rise of Arabi Pasha's nationalist movement led Britain to occupy Egypt in 1882, thus breaking the Anglo-French 'dual economic control' set up in 1878. While in Southern Africa, the rise of Boer nationalism also led to eventual British expansion. Other peripheral approaches have focused on the role of individual 'men on the spot' — such as Cecil Rhodes, who played a big part in events in Southern Africa — especially regarding the Boer states.

Finally, another approach is offered by 'International Relations' theorists, such as A. J. P. Taylor and Kennedy, who stress the role of inter-European rivalry and global developments. Fieldhouse at first took this view, but more recently has stressed the importance of economic problems in Africa as a 'pull' factor — a sort of peripheral interpretation.

In fact, the extract seems to do this, containing references in the first paragraph to an 'informal' empire (favoured by revisionists who stress continuity rather than a break after 1870); and, in the second paragraph, where he refers to the importance of investments in non-empire states, such as the Argentine (as pointed out by Cain and Hopkins). So, to conclude, the historian seems to be offering a metropolitan/Marxist interpretation, but one which also considers other factors as playing at least a minor role, and is therefore quite a balanced approach.

Examiner says:

The content is once again linked to the question, with specific comments about the extract and the historian's approach. Rosie is also spot on with a conclusion about what can be learned from the extract.

Examiner says

Rosie's answer:

▷ is relevant and puts forward accurate knowledge about the economic and social developments connected to the topic

▷ includes detailed and relevant references to the extract

▷ shows a clear understanding of the historical interpretations relevant to the topic, and makes references to alternative approaches/methods.

Introduction

This section comprises four case studies based upon the following Non-British History options available for examination in the OCR GCE A2 History specification B Unit F986:

1 Different approaches to the Crusades, 1095–1272

2 Different interpretations of witch-hunting in early modern Europe, c.1560–c.1660

3 Different American Wests, 1840–1900

4 Debates about the Holocaust

For each case study, there is a brief introductory commentary outlining the background to the range of approaches that have been taken to explaining the features of the topic being studied. This is followed by a series of extracts from the writings of historians and a few primary sources. This is not an exercise in source analysis and evaluation. You will need to consider why historians create different interpretations of the same events. The activities linked to the extracts and sources should help you to work on developing this ability for different interpretations.

Each case study surveys some of the major interpretations that historians have suggested in the ongoing quest to understand them. Over the years, each has been, and continues to be, a lively subject in which new evidence, new attitudes, new approaches and new questions asked have all contributed to produce ongoing reflection and reconsideration by historians.

Case study 1: Different approaches to the Crusades, 1095–1272

Introduction

The historical analysis of the Crusades is one of contemporary significance that continues to raise questions about the interface between competing cultures and challenges Eurocentric interpretations of the past.

Even the definition of the term itself presents problems, and it is from this basic point that some of the main conflicts in Crusade studies arise. On the whole, contemporaries had no real concept of 'Crusades' as such; they were referred to generally by Latin or vernacular terms that indicated a journey, often a journey to Jerusalem or some other significant Christian feature of the 'Holy Land'. The cross was not a formal badge for 'Crusades', as opposed to more general pilgrimage, until the end of the twelfth century. The term *Crozada* was not used until the early thirteenth century, and even then remained rare, while the English term 'Crusade' was not in common use until the eighteenth century. Interestingly, one fourteenth-century propagandist referred to crusading as 'the hunt of God'.

The nineteenth century saw the development of a romanticised view of the Crusades which fitted well with the struggle for the growth of empire, the revival of interest in everything medieval and the spreading of the Christian gospel to 'the poor native'. It was only in the twentieth century as western empires retreated that this began to be challenged.

Passage **1**   **The Crusade as an expression of Christian religious enthusiasm**

At rare moments of history the feeling of Christian fellowship overmasters the jealousies and hatreds by which the church of Christ is ever likely to be rent asunder. In the brilliant prospect of common action and common sacrifice for a cause held to be great and sacred, dividing memories are laid aside and petty suspicions discarded. That such an emotional experience was vouchsafed to the chivalry of Western Europe as it took the cross in response to the Pope's appeal is established by evidence that may be inferred from the probabilities. For the time had now come when Europe, which had so long been exposed to barbarian attacks could carry the war into the enemy quarters. The Saracens had been expelled from Sicily and Crete, the navies of Venice, Genoa and Pisa ruled the Mediterranean, the overland route to Constantinople had been opened.

It is also to be remembered that in France, which more than any other country was the soul of the Crusade, the Church had succeeded in giving to the military caste something of its own code of aspiration. The institution of chivalry, as it was developed at the end of the eleventh century, had the great merit of laying stress upon the responsibilities attaching to the possession of force. The young knight was initiated into his knighthood with all the solemnities which the pious imagination of those days could devise ... He was already, in all but name, enlisted as a Crusader.

The first military enterprise of united Europe was distinguished by its absence of organisation. The Crusaders who, in a wild fit of enthusiasm, left their homes for the east were empty of all that it most concerned them to know. They knew nothing of the geography, climate or population, were ignorant of hygiene and contemptuous of discipline.

H. A. L. Fisher (1935) A History of Europe, vol. 1, Eyre and Spottiswoode, pp. 224–5.

FOR DISCUSSION

In a small group, read passage 1 and discuss key words and phrases that suggest how Fisher seeks to explain the Crusades. Keep a record of these for later use in considering where Fisher's ideas might fit into later explanatory modes.

Most modern interpretations of the Crusades stem from Carl Erdmann's book, *Die Entstehung des Kreuzzugsgedankens* (1935), which shifted the focus of study to the origins of the Crusades. Erdmann was a theologian who combined a concentration on the ideas that underpinned the observable events of history with rigorous training in critical use of sources. Erdmann's view might fall within the general definition of a generalist interpretation. Generalists look for an explanation of the origins and nature of crusading in a long history of Christian holy war dating from long before the Crusades. They consider the importance of ideas like a '**just war**' and the significance of the ideal of Christian knighthood, which were developing in western Europe in particular in the tenth and eleventh centuries. In this context, the Crusades came to be understood as one group of episodes in a long-term line of thinking that produced a theoretical justification of warfare from a Christian perspective. From this perspective, there developed two major alternative views of the Crusades.

Just war

While the basic principles of Christianity opposed war, this idea was used to justify war in certain circumstances such as opposing ruthless and violent injustice.

Moors

Originally a Roman name for inhabitants of what is now Morocco, it is generally applied to the Muslim forces who invaded and occupied large parts of Spain between 711 and 1492.

The more restrictive interpretation of Crusades is that of the traditionalists for whom these are the essential features of a Crusade:

- It should be directed towards the Latin East.
- Its focus should be the liberation of the Holy Places from Muslim control.
- It should bring assistance to the Christians of the Holy Land suffering persecution and suppressed by Muslim rulers.

One of the earliest proponents of this view was Stephen Runciman whose work, *A History of the Crusades* (1951–4), has been described as 'The last great medieval chronicle'. Perhaps the most prominent traditionalist was H. E. Mayer, who defined a Crusade in his work *The Crusades* (1965) as a campaign with the goal of domination over the **Holy Sepulchre**. For traditionalists, the wars against Muslims in Spain or pagans in Northern Europe, even when conducted with papal approval, do not fall within the realm of study, so their analysis of the Crusades becomes a relatively limited field. For some traditionalists, only the first campaign to the Holy Land (1095–9) represents the true values of Crusade, though there is sometimes a differentiation between the official Crusade summoned by Pope Urban II and the popular Crusade launched by Peter the Hermit. For such traditionalists, the 'true' Crusades petered out after the Children's Crusade.

However, the idea that the Crusades sprang suddenly from the climactic sermon of Urban II at Clermont in 1095 might seem difficult to justify.

Passage (2) **Papal motivation**

From 1060 the reformed papacy applied their theories of justified war with even greater vigour and legal precision to campaigns against the infidel than they did to those against their Christian enemies ... Although it appears that many holy war aspects of the reconquest of Muslim Spain resulted from the First Crusade rather than the other way round, the Iberian peninsula attracted interest from Popes and French knights and fitted neatly and centrally into the increasingly grandiose concepts of worldly destiny being peddled not just by papal apologists but by monastic reformers as well. Glaber, a Cluniac Benedictine whose order had a long and close interest both in the Christian kingdoms of northern Spain and in promoting pilgrimage, peppered his chronicles with accounts of pilgrimages to Jerusalem (which he feared had become abused as a fashionable accessory for those seeking prestige not penitence); Christian warfare against the **Moors** in Spain and, on one occasion, the Slavs beyond the Elbe; and the 'Peace and Truce of God Movement'. Glaber was of no doubt of the efficacy of all of them: even monks who broke their vows and in extremis took up arms were seen as gaining salvation. In this context papal approval and grants of specific spiritual privileges to warriors against infidels would have occasioned little surprise.

Theories and practices of morally just and spiritually meritorious warfare had developed unevenly in response to changing political circumstances, religious outlook and social behaviour. Many clung to older concepts of sin and spiritual war. Some feigned or genuinely felt shocked at the unapologetic and unequivocal combination of war and penance proposed by Urban II in 1095. Yet the pre-history of the First Crusade was long and illustrious ... holy wars against infidels who, by the late eleventh century appeared, if not in retreat, then at least to be subject to attack on equal terms, provided one means of legitimate expression for a military aristocracy whose social authority and robust culture served to highlight their spiritual vulnerability.

The catalyst was as much to do with the perspectives and interests of the reformed papacy as the external threats presented by Islam: together they set the stage for Urban II. Yet much of what was proclaimed as new by the call to arms in 1095 represented old wine in new bottles.

C. Tyerman (2006) *God's War*, Penguin, pp. 55–7.

A more wide-ranging view of the Crusades begins from the basis that any campaign receiving support from the Pope against 'heretics, **schismatics** and other enemies of the Church' should be considered as a Crusade. Consequently, the definition of a Crusade can be extended to include campaigns against religious dissenters, pagans, Muslims and political opponents within Europe. For example, the destruction of the Knights Templar by Philip IV of France (1307–12) might even warrant consideration under this heading. This is known as the pluralist interpretation. The origins of his approach are generally attributed to Giles Constable's investigation of the Crusades in 1953 and it is best represented in the writings of Jonathan Riley-Smith.

> **What motivations for the first Crusade are suggested by passage 2? Identify ideas in this passage that might undermine the traditional view of the Crusades.**

Passage 3 A pluralist definition

[A Crusade was] a holy war authorised by the Pope who proclaimed it in the name of God or Christ … a defensive reaction to injury or aggression or as an attempt to recover Christian territories lost to the infidels. It answered the needs of the whole church or all of Christendom … rather than those of a particular nation.

J. Riley-Smith (1975) *What were the Crusades?*, Macmillan, p. 12.

Schismatics

A schism refers to a split in the unity of the Catholic church; a schismatic is someone who supports such a split.

Source A The Crusades, 1095–1250

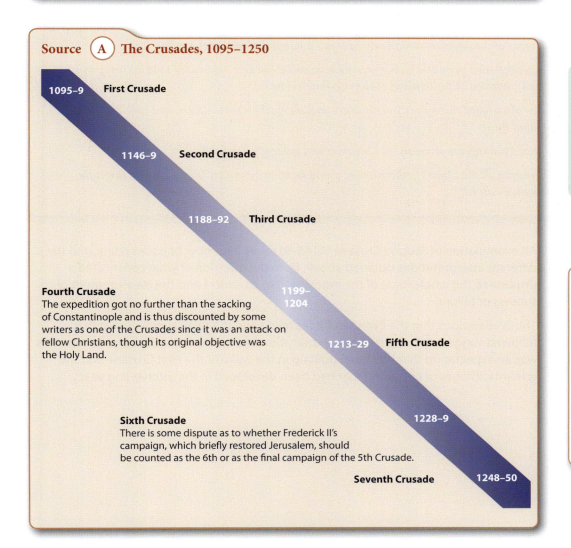

1095–9 First Crusade

1146–9 Second Crusade

1188–92 Third Crusade

Fourth Crusade
The expedition got no further than the sacking of Constantinople and is thus discounted by some writers as one of the Crusades since it was an attack on fellow Christians, though its original objective was the Holy Land.

1199–1204

1213–29 Fifth Crusade

Sixth Crusade
There is some dispute as to whether Frederick II's campaign, which briefly restored Jerusalem, should be counted as the 6th or as the final campaign of the 5th Crusade.

1228–9

Seventh Crusade **1248–50**

> **In what ways would you expect a timeline of the Crusades like that in source A to differ between the pluralist and the traditionalist interpretations?**

Stretch and challenge

Does the Fourth Crusade (1199–1204) fulfil any of the necessary criteria of a Crusade for a pluralist interpretation? Justify your decision.

Modern investigations of the Crusades have led to:

- increasingly diverse views of the role of Christian crusaders in the Middle East
- emphasis on the social and economic conditions in Europe that produced the crusading era (i.e. non-religious motives for Crusade and non-religious intentions and motivations of crusaders)
- the development of the idea that this was a medieval example of colonialism (the Outremer kingdoms representing an early manifestation of the planting of colonies in foreign territories).

Source B Key events of the Second Crusade	
December 1144	*The city and county of Edessa, most northerly of the Crusader states, fell to Zengi of Mosul*
Easter Sunday, 1146	*Bernard of Clairvaux launched the call to a new Crusade from Pope Eugenius III in the presence of King Louis VII of France and his queen, Eleanor of Aquitaine, at Vezelay in North Burgundy*
	Over the next year, Bernard toured Europe preaching the message and by spring 1147, tens of thousands had 'signed up'
Late summer of 1147	*The main armies of the Crusade arrived in Constantinople led by the Holy Roman Emperor, Conrad III (September) and Louis VII (October) of France, having travelled overland*
October 1147	*Conrad pressed ahead with his forces, only to be heavily defeated near Dorylaeum, losing most of his army and equipment and fleeing with just a handful of mounted knights*
	Louis proceeded more slowly, but was no more successful and in January 1148 his army was heavily defeated at the battle of Mount Cadmus (Homaz)
May 1148	*Louis abandoned the majority of his army, including all his foot soldiers, and sailed on to Syria without them*
Spring 1148	*Various contingents arrive in the Outremer and generally headed first for Jerusalem*
June 1148	*Eventually all the leaders gathered in Acre and together agreed on Damascus as a target for immediate attack*

An examination of Second Crusade (1146–9) raises a number of issues relating to the different interpretations outlined above, from the question of what constituted a Crusade to the whole issue of the motivation of crusaders and the measurement of success or failure.

The preparations that the Christian forces made and the tactical moves that they followed suggest that there was an expectation of a quick victory. To some extent, this was an expectation that had been built up in the wake of the First Crusade and the romantic images of crusading that had been developed in the intervening years.

Source **C** **The Outremer territories**

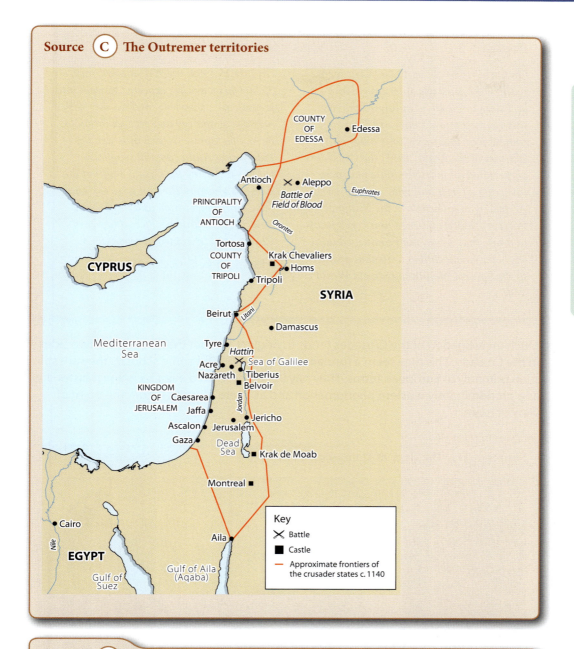

To what extent do sources B and C support the idea that the Crusades were not about defending the Holy Sepulchre to allow access to Christian pilgrims, but more about the seizing and holding of colonial territories in a predominantly hostile region?

Passage **4** **The legacy of the First Crusade**

Within a decade a first generation of texts had been created in northern and southern France, the Rhineland, Bavaria, Italy and Spain. Under the over-arching framework of God's guiding hand the deeds of bold warriors came to the fore: 'No matter how much the terrible glint of [enemy] arms glittered from innumerable columns, the splendour of their courage would still outdo it if it were visible, they marched out to fight with one mind – not to flee, but to die or win.'

Everyone who had taken part wanted their role to be immortalised and families had a huge sense of pride in the achievements of individuals of their clan. The standing of Geoffrey of Bouillon, for example was immense ... in the aftermath of the First Crusade the crusader's standing was such that the King of France was happy to offer Bohemund, probably the leading military figure, the hand in marriage of his eldest daughter.

J. Phillips (2007) 'Crusade superheroes', in *BBC History Magazine*, vol. 8(8), August.

Which interpretation(s) of Crusades might be supported by this analysis of the First Crusade? Highlight key issues that might be developed to support one interpretation of the Crusades and undermine others.

To what extent do the views expressed in passage 5 represent a departure from other interpretations of the Crusades?

Passage 5

On June 7 1099 about 40,000 Crusaders reached the outskirts of Jerusalem and laid siege to the city. On July 15 the city was stormed and a frenzy of killing commenced. According to [Philip] Hitti [*History of the Arabs*, 1937] the Crusaders perpetrated an indiscriminate massacre involving all ages and both sexes. According to an article in the National Post they 'killed unarmed non-combatants at a rate that would not be matched until the Nazi mobile killing units that operated in the Soviet Union in the Second World War' ...

On July 15 1999, the 900th anniversary, 2,000 Christians are expected to walk into Jerusalem ... they will enter the city with a message of apology and reconciliation to be met by representatives of Israel, the Palestinian Authority and religious leaders including the Grand Mufti of the Al Aqsa Mosque. The aim is 'to ask and pray for reconciliation and forgiveness and clean the historically bad image of Christianity in a spirit of repentance'.

F. Kutty, *Revisiting the Crusades*, 15 July 1999.

Much investigation of the Crusades tends to neglect the fact that there were two sides in the Crusade. This may seem a fundamental point, but for some scholars they are still seen primarily in European terms. They have been described even by Islamist historians as a predominantly western phenomenon and as 'mere pinpricks' from the point of view of Islam.

Source D   The siege of Damascus, 1148

An illustration from a fifteenth-century Flemish manuscript

Source (E) From the Muslim account of the siege of Damascus

After a fierce struggle the **Franks** *overwhelmed the Muslims, seized the water supplies and camped in the gardens around the city. They closed in on the city closer than any army had ever been. The population were disheartened and uncertain what to do, but at dawn on the Sunday the army made a sortie, attacked the Franks and defeated them, killing and wounding large numbers …*

Meanwhile letters had been sent to the provincial governor to ask for help. Turcoman cavalry and infantry from the *province poured into the area and in the morning, reinforced and heartened the Muslims returned to the battle …*

News reached the Franks from many sources that the Muslims were bearing down on them to attack … and they felt their defeat was certain. They decided the only way to escape the trap was to take flight and at dawn the following Wednesday they retreated in miserable confusion and disorder.

Ibn al-Qalanisi, 1160, quoted in F.Gabrieli (1989) *Arab Historians of the Crusades,* Dorset Press, pp. 56–9.

Franks

Generic term used by Muslims to describe all western crusaders.

BIOGRAPHY

Ibn al-Qalanisi (c. 1070–1160) was an official and politician in Damascus. His *Continuation of the Chronicle of Damascus* is one of the very few contemporary sources for the Second Crusade from the point of view of a Muslim.

How far do passage 5 and sources D and E contribute to the justification of an alternative Islamic view of the Crusades?

After the retreat from Damascus, even though the allied forces remained largely intact, support for further campaigning crumbled, and Conrad quickly abandoned the Crusade, accusing local leaders of deceiving him. He returned to Germany while Louis stayed on through the winter before finally departing for France after Easter 1149.

But the second Crusade was much more complex than this. Such was the success of Bernard of Clairvaux's recruitment drive that the Pope decided to open a further front against the Muslims in Moorish Spain and Bernard allowed another group of 'crusaders' to fulfil their pledge in a campaign against the pagans beyond the eastern border of the Holy Roman Empire in the Baltic region.

In the late summer of 1147, a significant group of crusaders from northern Europe and England set sail to reach the Holy Land by sea. Seeking to link up with King Alfonso Enriques of Portugal, they helped him to besiege the city of Lisbon. After some negotiations between spokesmen of the various groups and the king, Alfonso announced that those who remained with him at the siege could seize whatever goods and possessions of the enemy they might find if the campaign was successful and claim the ransom money from any prisoners of status whose families were prepared to pay for their release. In addition, those who chose to remain after the capture of the city should have a share of the conquered land according to their rank.

The outcome represented the only real success of the whole Second Crusade – after a siege of nearly 17 weeks, the Moors surrendered the city to the forces led by Alfonso Enriques.

Consider how source F might be used to justify the claims of two different interpretations of the Crusades.

Source (F) A contemporary chronicler describes the surrender of Lisbon

The Archbishop and the other bishops went in front of us with the Lord's cross and then our leaders entered together with the King and those who had been selected. How everyone rejoiced! What great joy and what a great abundance there was of pious tears when, to the praise and honour of God and of the most Holy Virgin Mary, the saving cross was placed atop the highest tower to be seen by all as a symbol of the city's subjection.

The men of Cologne and the Flemings … did not observe their oaths. They plundered. They broke down doors … destroyed clothes and utensils … treated virgins shamefully …

The Normans and English, however, for whom faith and religion were of the greatest importance … remained quietly in their assigned positions, preferring to stay their hands from looting rather than violate the obligations of their faith and their oathbound association …

Osbernus, *De Expugnatione Lyxbonensi, 1147*, quoted in the Internet Medieval Sourcebook, Fordham University Center for Medieval Studies.

Attempts to recreate the essence of the Crusades has taxed the film industry, from romantic portrayals of Richard the Lionheart to more 'gritty' interpretations like the Ridley Scott production, 'Kingdom of Heaven' (2005).

1. Is film ever useful in helping to demonstrate historical interpretation?

2. Is Professor Riley-Smith's criticism of 'Kingdom of Heaven' reasonable or excessive?

Passage 6 Film as history

Set between the Second and Third Crusades at the time of the rise of Saladin and the loss of Jerusalem to the united forces of Islam, the film 'Kingdom of Heaven' was billed as:

'A spectacular saga of courage passion and adventure. Amidst the pageantry and intrigue of medieval Jerusalem a young blacksmith having lost everything, finds honour and redemption on a valiant quest. Against staggering odds he battles overwhelming forces to save his people and fulfil his destiny.' ('Kingdom of Heaven', DVD cover notes, 2005)

Professor of ecclesiastical history, Jonathan Riley-Smith was less lyrical however, claiming that the plot was:

'… complete and utter nonsense. [Riley-Smith] said that it relied on a dramatised view of the Crusades propagated by Sir Walter Scott in his book The Talisman published in 1825 and now discredited by academics … "Its rubbish. It's not historically accurate at all. They refer to The Talisman which depicts the Muslims as sophisticated and civilised, and the Crusaders are all brutes and barbarians. It has nothing to do with reality." … Dr Jonathan Philips, a lecturer in history … agreed that the film relied on an outdated portrayal of the Crusades and could not be described as "a history lesson".' (C. Edwardes, 'Ridley Scott's new Crusades film "panders to Osama bin Laden"', Telegraph.co.uk, 17 January 2004)

Stretch and challenge

In a small group, compare 'Kingdom of Heaven' (2005) with any other film about the Crusades that you can find. Explain the differences in interpretation.

Conclusion

Almost every aspect of the Crusades has been subject to question in the last 50 years. Even in the early twentieth century, the Crusades still tended to be viewed almost as a contemporary issue with Muslims, pagans, heretics and other outside groups being seen as a threat, real or imagined, to western civilisation. In the late nineteenth century, this was, however, beginning to change, with a growing tendency to view the Crusades with either aversion or admiration and nostalgia. Since then, further re-interpretations have been influenced by the desires to relate these conflicts to the modern world and move away from an imperialist and/or a strictly Eurocentric interpretation. Today, as in the past, the Crusades continue to be interpreted in the light of the different positions from which they have been analysed.

> Go back to the work you did on passage 1 and consider where you would place Fisher's interpretation in the spectrum of views of the Crusades. Highlight words or phrases from the passage that justify your decision.

THINK LIKE AN HISTORIAN

Re-read the case study about the underlying causes of the Crusades, and work through the questions that follow:

(a) What can you learn from passage 2 about the interpretations, approaches and methods of this historian? Refer to the extract and your knowledge to explain your answer.

EXAM TIP

When answering question (a), you will need to do *two* things:

(i)   Support your answer by *detailed* reference to the extract AND refer to alternative approaches/methods.

(ii) Use relevant and accurate knowledge as part of a thorough analysis of the interpretation.

(b) Some historians apply the term 'Crusade' only to those campaigns directed by the Pope towards the recovery or defence of the holy sites of Christianity in Jerusalem and the Holy Land. What are its limitations in explaining the religious campaigns launched by the Christian Church between 1095 and 1291?

EXAM TIP

As with (a) questions, you will have to do *two* things to achieve a top grade in (b) questions:

(i)   Show both advantages and disadvantages/shortcomings of the approach/method, AND compare it with other approaches/methods.

(ii) Use relevant and accurate knowledge to assess both advantages *and* disadvantages.

EXAM TIP

In looking at different interpretations of the past, it is important to understand the reasons for these differences. You will need to ask yourself questions like those posed in this case study. As well as helping you to decide on your own interpretation of events, this should help you to understand how and why different historians have come to their conclusions, and how their alternative arguments might be supported and sustained. Equally, it should help you to point out any drawbacks and/or weakness in their interpretations.

THINK LIKE AN HISTORIAN continued

EXAM TIP

Before submitting your answer to the questions above and moving on to the next case study, use the checklist below to make sure you have taken the right approach for a top grade.

If this is your own book, put ticks in the boxes as appropriate. Remember, the job isn't done until all the boxes have been filled.

Key areas checklist

Knowledge and understanding	Understanding of approaches/methods	Evaluation of approaches/methods
To tick this box, you need to show/use some precise additional own knowledge about events and developments relevant to the topic, and show awareness and understanding of issues relating to the available evidence.	To tick this box, you need to understand the nature of the different approaches used by historians, and the reasons for this (e.g. personal beliefs about what history is, the influence of contemporary events, the type/nature of evidence available and the questions asked of it).	To tick this box, you need to be able to show you are aware of the strengths and weaknesses of the various approaches/interpretations relevant to the topic, e.g. what can be learned from one approach that cannot be gained from others; how different perspectives on the debates provide different answers to the questions asked; whether the different interpretations can be combined to produce a synthesis.
Achieved?	Achieved?	Achieved?

EXAM TIP

When starting to investigate different historical interpretations and evaluations of witch-hunting in early modern Europe, make sure you go beyond a 'labels'/ school of thought approach. Instead, try to examine closely the evidence that the various historians have used, and think about the strengths/ weaknesses of each of their approaches as well as their interpretations.

Case study 2: Different interpretations of witch-hunting in early modern Europe, c. 1560–c. 1660

Introduction

A study of witch-hunting across Europe raises many anomalies which may provide support for different and sometimes conflicting interpretations of both the scale of and motivation for witch-hunting. Nowhere are the anomalies more clearly found than in the region identified by many as the centre of the witch-hunting craze, the lands of the Holy Roman Empire and those adjacent lands with significant Germanic populations.

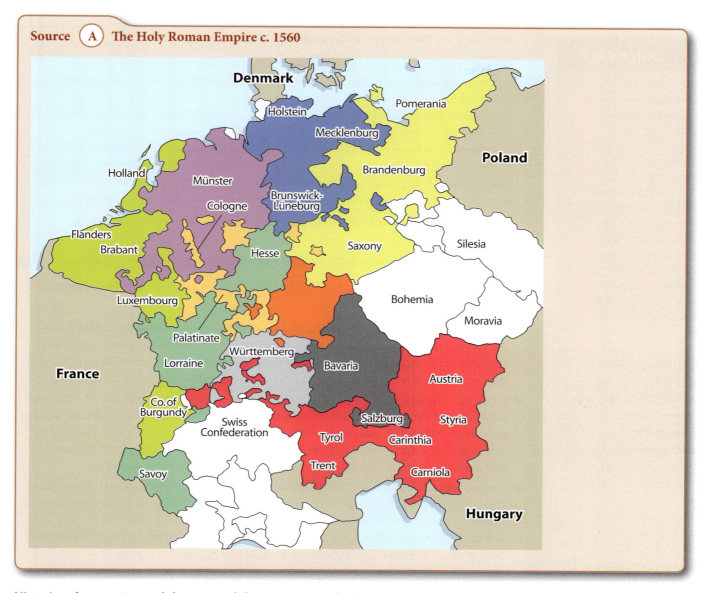

Historians have estimated that around three-quarters of all witchcraft executions took place in this region, although the actual number is still hotly debated. Brian Levack (*The Witch Hunt in Early Modern Europe* (2006)) estimates that some 60,000 witches died throughout Europe, while Ronald Hutton ('Counting the Witch Hunt', an unpublished essay) disputes this, suggesting 40,000 executions; both estimates are based on reasoned statistical analysis. Both challenged Anne Llewellyn Barstow (*Witchcraze* (1995)) and her figure of 100,000 or more executions. Early estimates reached into the millions, but these were largely based on guesswork founded on the statement in much early literature of witch-hunting that 'lots of witches' died and on sensationalised accounts based on Lamoth Langon's *Histoire de l'Inquisition en France* (1829). Now largely discounted as a forgery, Langon's work was the foundation of most studies of witchcraft up to the 1970s.

There are also difficulties studying witchcraft in a specific region such as Germany; it was not a unified state and suffered wide divisions based on religion, government, social structure, economics and other more localised factors. It was quite possible for an extreme witch-hunt to be raging like fire through one community while, not far away, an apparently serious witchcraft case failed to produce even a single execution.

QUICK FACT

In Germany, in particular, there was a crossover between witch craze and antisemitism. Sacred Hebrew terms were often used and corrupted beyond their original meaning. The great gatherings of witches that took place were originally referred to as 'synagogues', later **sabbats** (or Sabbaths) – the Jewish day of rest.

What issues does a problem like the one in passage 1 raise for any approach to the investigation of witch-hunting?

LINK UP

'From above' and 'from below' interpretations – see Chapter 1, p. 17.

Passage ① The nature of the problem

In times of severe panic usual limitations could be breached and all manner of men and women could be accused. Where torture was used, as it commonly was, to provide names of others who had been with them at the 'sabbat', a chain reaction was set in progress that could deliver into the hands of witch judges persons of considerable prominence and respectability. Such was the experience of the city of Ellberg in south-west Germany. Starting with a woman of 70, who was tortured into confessing, many people were executed after being forced into naming accomplices. In 1611 some 100 were executed and 160 the following year. A judge who protested when his wife was accused and executed was himself tortured and executed in 1611. Executions continued at a reduced rate until 1618.

G. Scarre and J. Callow (2nd edition, 2001) *Witchcraft and Magic in Sixteenth- and Seventeenth-Century Europe*, Palgrave, pp. 31–2.

The witch-hunt in Ellberg in south-west Germany shares several features with witch-hunts elsewhere. For example:

- The hunt began with the accusation of an elderly woman. Some historians have suggested that elderly women were easy victims in times of economic and social uncertainty. A more extreme view points to anti-feminist sentiment in which it was easiest to begin with those women who were least able to defend themselves.

- Once accusations had been made, it seemed impossible to stop them. The basis of such accusations included personal rivalries within the community, with the witch-hunt being used as a means of settling individual grievances, or an attempt by the authorities to impose their will on the masses, in which they approved the use of torture as a means of gaining the assent of the masses to their authority.

- Anyone could be accused. This might suggest that the witch-hunt was driven from the bottom up not from the top down; that the authorities were powerless to resist popular pressure in particular circumstances; and in order to maintain their authority, the authorities gave in to this pressure, even sacrificing members of their own group if necessary, to help them keep some degree of control.

In 1969, a new phase in 'witch craze' scholarship began with the publication of Hugh Trevor-Roper's study, *The European Witchcraze of the Sixteenth and Seventeenth Centuries*. This launched a new phase of scholarship that progressively undermined earlier theories. One of these discarded theories was that of nineteenth-century historian Michelet whose thesis was based on the idea of a bottom-up revolt against church authority leading to repressive control from those authorities of any manifestations of devil worship or black masses. Likewise discredited was Margaret Murray's theory that witchcraft (or paganism) was the natural religion of the European peasant throughout the Middle Ages until the Reformation finally swept it away. Murray was an Egyptologist who believed that this paganistic belief could be traced from a Roman fertility cult and that events like the burning of Joan of Arc were manifestations of this, a form of ritual sacrifice. The main problem with Murray's work was that it simply ignored evidence, or rather the lack of it. There is little evidence of anything more than a few fragmentary survivals of paganistic rituals and even these were often practised in parallel with a Christian approach to specific personal and local problems like crop failure.

Passage 2 The development of witch craze studies

Although historians have long taken an interest in early modern beliefs in witchcraft and magic and their terrible consequences for those involved, the past 30 years have witnessed an explosion of scholarly interest. One important feature of much of this writing has been the substantial use of techniques from across discipline boundaries. Anthropologists, sociologists and feminist theorists have all brought their different skills, talent and insight to bear on our understanding of historical phenomena ... leading scholars have undertaken painstaking research of court records and other archival material relating to both accusers and accused. [As a result] an altogether more sophisticated picture of the intellectual and social basis for witch theory has begun to emerge replacing many of the previously held assumptions about the nature of witchcraft and rationale behind its prosecution.

G. Scarre and J. Callow (2001), p. 2.

To appreciate more fully the ways in which different approaches might lead to very different views of what was happening in the Germanic lands in the sixteenth and seventeenth centuries, it can help to consider different possible responses to specific cases like the ones that follow.

Passage 3 The case of Ursula Fladin, 1581–6

In 1581 in the parish of Durrenthal in Saxony the sixty-year-old wife of a linen weaver was subjected to a charge of sorcery and four main testimonies were placed against her ranging from causing diarrhoea to harming cattle and divination, cases that ranged over the previous nine years. The investigating judge referred the case to a higher court at Leipzig, which gave permission for the next stage, torture, to be applied. However Fladin admitted nothing damaging and her family had meantime set about destroying the case about her and in June the court in Leipzig recommended her release.

However this was not the end of the case: in 1582 she was again arrested, for godless behaviour, whilst her family was pursuing a counter claim for wrongful arrest, imprisonment and torture against the original judge.

R. Scribner (1990) 'Witchcraft and judgement in Reformation Germany', in *History Today*, April, pp. 13–4.

Passage 4 The case of Else Wessensee, 1536

In 1536 [Else Wessensee] was arrested on a charge of sorcery laid by her local community at Blankenhain in Saxony. The district governor had her imprisoned and interrogated and she initially named two accomplices but then retracted this and the governor decided she should be released. However her local community was not satisfied and demanded her torture. When she still protested her innocence in front of witnesses from her local community, the governor released her.

R. Scribner (1990), pp. 15–6.

FOR DISCUSSION

In a small group, discuss the difference between 'anthropologists, sociologists and feminist theorists'. Try to think of ways in general that their different purposes might affect their approach to the explanation of witch-hunts. What might be the strengths and weaknesses of using such approaches in the study of historical issues?

LINK UP

History and anthropology – see Chapter 2, p. 39.

History as a social science – see Chapter 2, p. 25.

Feminist history – see Chapter 1, p. 19.

Passages 3 and 4 and source B describe three different cases of witchcraft prosecutions.

Consider how two different approaches to witchcraft might lead to different interpretations and conclusions about these cases.

List the advantages and disadvantages of using each of your chosen approaches in investigating these cases.

Source ⓑ The witch-hunt at Eichstat, 1637

'*Monday 15 November 1637*

[After questioning before the court] She was then taken to the torture chamber and subjected to the strapado.

After being hoisted up a little she says that yes she could be a witch yet when released she announces she is not a witch. Therefore she is pulled up higher and then a second and third time and then released on admission that she is a witch, but immediately she becomes stubborn and denies she is a witch (the fourth time she is left hanging until a full confession has been extracted and after agreeing that all she has said is true is led away).'

Quoted in B. Levack (2004) *The Witchcraft Sourcebook*, Routledge, p 203.

The above cases deal with some of the explanations that have been offered for the witch craze. As an historian, it is up to you to examine the reasons that might have led scholars to place emphasis on different elements of the actual events when trying to explain the outburst of witch-hunting in the sixteenth and seventeenth centuries.

While the examples above will provide support for several different approaches, all historians must justify any interpretation with as wide a range of evidence as possible. To this end, you might consider whether the contemporary illustrations shown in sources C and D shed further light on the possible causes of such outbreaks. These illustrations introduce two potentially new elements.

1. How might source C have contributed to the sixteenth- and seventeenth-century obsession with witches?

2. Does the feminist approach have any advantages in interpreting the causes of witch-crazes? What are its weaknesses as a way of looking at this problem?

Source ⓒ 'The Angry Wife', an engraving, 1495

In 'The Angry Wife', by Israel van Meckenham, the woman uses a distaff, a tool used in spinning (a woman's job) to beat the man in a quarrel over 'who wears the trousers' – his breeches are on the floor in front of him. A demon hovers over them.

'*The Power of Women*' was a popular theme of northern European Art during the Renaissance. This was not, as its name might infer, an early form of feminism, but rather the reverse, a misogynistic response to rapid social change. The idea of the power of women and the whole concept of the overturning of 'the natural order of things' provided entertainment and was the root of a whole industry in satirical prints that could be reproduced cheaply and circulated widely for the enjoyment of a population who could identify with the images even if they were barely literate. As the tensions of the Reformation began to ease, such images lost their popularity as women ceased to be seen as an evil threat to mankind. This image is not specifically associated with witchcraft, yet it lends itself to the arguments of those taking a feminist approach to the issue of witch persecution.

Source (D) **'Thou shalt not suffer a witch to live'**

The burning of witches in 1574

Source D highlights the religious motivation of some of those who sought to expose witches. 'Thou shalt not suffer a witch to live' (The Holy Bible, 1611 (Exodus 22:18)) was taken from a long list of rules about moral behaviour that were part of the Old Testament story of the development of the Jewish people. The Protestant Reformation led to a wholesale re-examination of the Bible and fresh interpretations of its importance in everyday life. However, as Reformation and counter-Reformation developed, it became clear that the idea of the role of the devil was undergoing a re-evaluation. The whole study of demonology changed the way in which witches and their supposed activities were viewed.

In this context, it is unsurprising that some modern studies of the witch craze have approached the whole question through religion and have seen the phenomenon as a function of the conflict between Protestant and Catholic doctrines. This was partly the interpretation of Hugh Trevor-Roper, who suggested that witch-hunting was a conscious attack on Protestantism, pointing out that the rise in witch-hunts in the Holy Roman Empire coincided with the dominance of the Catholic forces of the Emperor. However, this interpretation is weakened by other evidence.

> ### Passage (5) The significance of religion
>
> *The most horrifying attacks in the German lands were made in the Catholic territories. Though the new Protestant magistrates also prosecuted for witchcraft they did not keep up with the prince-bishops and archbishop-electors, executing one witch to the Catholics three. At Trier between 1587 and 1593, 368 witches were burned from 22 villages ... at Eichstatt 274 persons were burned at the stake apparently in one year 1629.*
>
> *The fierce religious differences added another point of instability. Lutheran theologians stressed a demonology different from that of the Catholics. They taught that misfortune was caused by God's providence and that the devil did not have the enormous power with which popular belief credited [him]. Although traditional demonology still existed in Protestant minds, enabling Protestant magistrates to send many victims to their deaths, still, the new teaching had the effect of moderating the witch hunt in most Protestant lands.*
>
> A. Llewellyn Barstow (1995) *Witchcraze: New History of the European Witch Hunts*, HarperCollins, pp. 59–60.

For economic and social historians, the religious conflicts just provide the excuse for actions that basically stemmed from entirely different problems.

> ### Passage (6) Economic, social and demographic developments in early modern Europe
>
> *There is no question that some of the economic, social and demographic developments in early modern Europe aggravated the personal tensions that underlay many witch accusations. Inflation, an increase in poverty, pressure by a growing population on a limited supply of resources, the growth of the unattached female population and changes in the structure of the family all played some part in encouraging witchcraft accusation. Some women may have been accused of witchcraft because they were most adversely affected by such change, or with respect to the advent of capitalism, most resistant to it.*
>
> *In addition specific economic crises, such as famine, outbreaks of epidemic disease and dislocation caused by war, may have helped to trigger many individual witch-hunts. Wolfgang Behring has demonstrated a correlation between intense periods of witch hunting and harsh climatic conditions that produced widespread famine. Witch-hunts in Bavaria conform fairly closely to this pattern, but in other parts of Europe the connection is less apparent. Moreover many of the personal conflicts that led to witch accusations such as illness or the death of a young child were constant features of village life.'*
>
> B. Levack (2006) *The Witch-hunt in Early Modern Europe*, Pearson Education, p. 163.

LINK UP

Social and economic history – see Chapter 2, p. 32.

Passage 7 Explaining the witch craze

People in the 16th century were accustomed to using a wide range of differentiations when addressing matters of magic, sorcery and witchcraft. A person could engage in sorcery without being accused of witchcraft while an accusation of witchcraft could be met with both official and public scepticism. Popular hostility against an uncomfortable individual could pressure magistrates into burning someone as a witch but the way in which a witchcraze developed may have involved many other diverse factors outside the range of witch beliefs.

The persecution of witches was perhaps made possible because witchcraft could be appropriated for complex power games within early modern communities, but this was not always a matter of magistrates exploitatively imposing their will on cowed subjects: on the other hand witch trials were unthinkable without the collaboration of wide sections of the local community who could force magistrates to act against their better judgement.

It is clear that witch crazes did not arise because people were irrational, nor decline because they began to behave more rationally, like us. The pathological model of witchcraft appeals because it allows us a smug feeling of superiority that we really know 'what was wrong' with the people of a past age. The phenomenon of witchcrazes presupposed a distinctive understanding of the relationship between the sacred and the profane in which the Devil was an active force and magic and sorcery were possible forms of intervention to change the world. However they were also used rationally as part of deliberate strategies of survival, as weapons in communal politics and as ploys in complex power games.

R. Scribner (1990), p. 19.

Conclusion

It is important to remember that not all approaches to the issue of witch persecutions are covered in this brief survey. For example, the anthropological approach adopted by Thomas and McFarlane to show that witchcraft was about seeking to establish some sort of status in village society for the poor and excluded would need to be considered in a more detailed analysis, and only limited consideration has been given to psychological models of the witch craze. It is, however, important to recognise that there is now a great diversity of explanation of the place of the witch-hunt in European History and that all of these approaches have their supporters and detractors whose arguments are based on studying the same evidence, but with a different point of view or emphasis or, at root, a different process for the selection of sources to support a specific interpretation.

> **LINK UP**
>
> *Psychoanalytical history – see Chapter 2, p. 37.*

> **THINK LIKE AN HISTORIAN**
>
> Re-read the case study about the origins of witch-hunting in early modern Europe, and work through the two questions that follow.
>
> (a) What can you learn from passage 6 about the interpretations, approaches and methods of this historian? Refer to the extract and your knowledge to explain your answer.

THINK LIKE AN HISTORIAN *continued*

EXAM TIP

When answering question (a), you will need to do *two* things:

(i) Support your answer by *detailed* reference to the extract AND refer to alternative approaches/methods.

(ii) Use relevant and accurate knowledge as part of a thorough analysis of the interpretation.

(b) Some historians have focused on religious changes to explain the phenomenon of the European witch craze in the sixteenth and early seventeenth centuries. Explain how this has contributed to our understanding of witch-hunting. Has this approach any disadvantages or shortcomings?

EXAM TIP

As with (a) questions, you will have to do *two* things to achieve a top grade in (b) questions:

(i) Show both advantages and disadvantages/shortcomings of the approach/method, AND compare it with other approaches/methods.

(ii) Use relevant and accurate knowledge to assess both advantages *and* disadvantages.

EXAM TIP

Before submitting your answer to the questions above and moving on to the next case study, use the checklist on page 92 to make sure you have taken the right approach for a top grade.

Case study 3: Different American Wests, 1840–1900

Introduction

One of the first issues in the investigation of different approaches to the American West is the question of what constitutes 'the West'.

For some American historians, 'the West' begins at the Mississippi; for others, it begins with the eastern edge of 'the Plains' or at the Rockies, while some studies exclude the Pacific coastlands from 'the West' claiming that they are beyond the West. For the Spanish settlers in central America, 'the West' was 'the North' while for the British in Canada, it was 'the South'. Though such differences might sound trivial, they nonetheless underpin different approaches to what the West was, which, in turn, reflects on the way the history of the West is interpreted.

EXAM TIP

When starting to investigate different historical interpretations and evaluations of the different American Wests, make sure you go beyond a 'labels'/ school of thought approach. Instead, try to examine closely the evidence that the various historians have used, and think about the strengths/ weaknesses of each of their approaches as well as their interpretations.

Passage (1) Defining the West

Where the West begins depends on when you asked the question. In the 19th century Charles Dickens got no further than St Louis, nine hundred miles short of the Rockies. He went home convinced he had seen the West and declared it to be a fraud. In the 17th century the West began practically at the Atlantic seashore. It was synonymous with 'the frontier', that inland danger line where the colonial settlement ended and the woods and the Indians started. In the coastal towns of Massachusetts a fond father, seeing his daughter off on a journey of only 15 miles to visit relatives wrote in his diary 'I greatly fear for Abigail's safety … it is her first journey into the West, and I shall pray mightily for her return.'

In the time of **Jefferson** *the West was anywhere beyond the crest of the Appalachians.*

A. Cooke (1977) *Alistair Cooke's America*, BBC Books, p. 156.

Source (A) Westward expansion in the USA

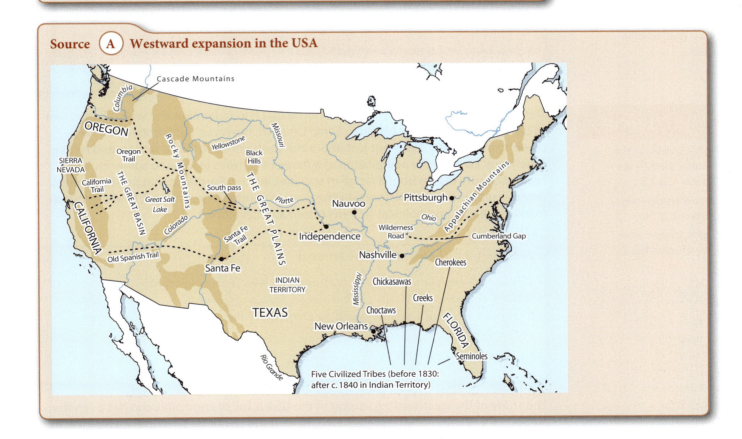

QUICK FACT

Thomas Jefferson was the third President of the USA (1801–9).

FOR DISCUSSION

Does it matter where 'the West' begins and what it does or doesn't include? How might this affect approaches to explaining and analysing the West?

Frontier

Generally defined as the boundary between the settled East and the unsettled 'West' of America. 'Closing the Frontier' was used by Turner to suggest that all the available land had been explored and brought within the boundaries of the USA – that the West had been 'tamed', an idea that is itself open to debate.

LINK UP

Profound causes – the 'Frontier thesis' – see Chapter 1, p. 12.

Cultural history – see Chapter 2, p. 36.

Empirical approaches – see Chapter 1, p. 7.

Alongside the issue of where the West begins stands the question of 'the **Frontier**'. In 1890, the American historian Frederick Jackson Turner in declaring the Frontier to be closed, defined it as the meeting point between civilisation and savagery, equating savagery in nineteenth-century terms with the existence and independence of the Native American tribes.

The concept was formally expressed shortly after the 'closing of the Frontier' in 1890 by Turner speaking at a meeting of historians at the World's Columbian Exhibition in Chicago in 1893 on 'The significance of the Frontier in American History'.

Source **A** **Turner's thesis**

Up to our own day American History has been in a large degree the history of the colonisation of the Great West. The existence of an area of free land, its continuous recession and the advance of settlement westward, explain American development … (but now) … four centuries from the discovery of America, at the end of a hundred years of life under the Constitution, the frontier has gone and with it has closed the first period of American History

Frederick Jackson Turner speaking at a meeting of historians at the World's Columbian Exhibition in Chicago in 1893, quoted in R. V. Hine and J. M. Faragher (2000) *The American West: A New Interpretive History,* Yale University Press, pp. 493–4.

The Frontier was a region of conflict, a battle that had to be won and which Turner saw as having been 'won'. For historian Sarah Deutsch, however, the Frontier was the meeting of cultures. It was not just about the clash between white settlers and Native Americans, but was the assimilation of a range of cultures leading to a new multi-layered culture drawn from a range of societies and backgrounds that itself became a unique culture. Frontier history tells the story of communities created, land exploited, markets created and political systems tested and developed.

Passage **2** **The history of the Frontier**

Whatever its boundaries in American History, the West is not only a modern region somewhere beyond the Mississippi, but also the process of getting there. The history of the frontier is a unifying American theme, for every part of the country was once a frontier, every region 'the West'.

R. V. Hine and J. M. Faragher (2000), p. 11.

The study of the westward expansion of the USA is full of anomalies and has been the subject of a number of interpretations. One of these might be termed the empirical approach, which points to the mass migrations by European settlers during this period – from the Boers' trek out of the English-dominated Cape Colony in South Africa, driven by the British anti-slavery attitude, to Irish mass emigration, largely to the United States, as a result of the potato famine. Taken to its extreme, the empirical approach becomes particularist, suggesting that no single explanation is possible because each pioneer had their own particular reason for undertaking the hazardous journey west. However, there is substantial evidence of European populations moving in groups into the West. In the latter half of the nineteenth century, immigrants from Europe established hundreds of new communities in the West, often on land confiscated from Native American Indians. After the Civil War (1861–5), some states even pursued active immigrant recruitment policies sending out guides in different languages to potential European immigrants.

Passage 3 Westward expansion

The Irish offer one example. Often they came west as miners. At the end of the [nineteenth] century the copper centre of Butte (Montana) was the most Irish city in America and Butte miners told the joke of the Irishman who sent a letter home encouraging his brother to come over. 'Don't stop in the United States,' he wrote, 'come right on out to Butte'.

R. V. Hine and J. M. Faragher (2000), p. 383.

Those who support the 'thirst for exploration' theory argue that the mid-Victorian period saw an urge to discovery that was unparalleled in recent history. Such an argument might appear even more valid if extended to technological and scientific 'discovery' as well as the urge to discover new lands, but the motive for exploration and that for settlement do not necessarily coincide. Support for this approach might be found by looking at the significance of key individuals in the history of the American West, from Daniel Boone who first explored the westward route through the Appalachians and into the forested lands of Missouri beyond, to Buffalo Bill Cody and the populist image created by his Wild West Show. The West might then be seen as a story of individual exploration and enterprise.

Psychological factors have been cited in interpretations, which suggest that a search for structural explanations, dependent on the specific features of the government and society of the growing USA as a major factor in the popularity of moving West, are pointless because the '… the westward urge is a human instinct like the need to love or to taste spring air and believe again that life is not a dead end after all' (D. Lavender (1963) *Westward Vision: the Story of the Oregon Trail*, p. 26).

A further interpretation puts forward the idea that uprooting family and leaving behind the familiar to undertake the hazardous journey westwards in search of a new start was a specific manifestation of the unique American culture which included a permanent restlessness and need to escape. This was underpinned by the American understanding of the nature of liberty that was firmly enshrined in the Constitution. This can be demonstrated through an examination of the demography of those who travelled in the early wagon trains west. Many were newly married couples and often wives were pregnant for at least part of the journey.

LINK UP

Pyschoanalytical interpretations – see Chapter 1, p. 18.

Structural interpretations – see Chapter 1, p. 12.

Passage 4 The urge to move West

… this notion of restlessness receives ample support from the diaries, memoirs and recollections of the pioneers of the 1840s. The Plainsman James Clyman noted that it was a peculiarly American thing for people with comfortable homes in Missouri and elsewhere to set out for the unknown. The Sager family set out for Oregon largely because of the restlessness of the head of the household. The emigrant Mary J. Cummins gives a clear example of itchy-footedness which comes close to neurotic. She relates how she returned to her Illinois home on a Friday evening and found her mother with a long face. 'What do you think father had done?' her mother asked. 'I don't know' she replied. 'He has sold the farm and as soon as school closes we are moving to Missouri'. Needless to say Missouri did not suit either and the family was soon on its way to Oregon.

Part of this restlessness may be that the American farmer was a completely different kind of animal from the European peasant who looked on land as a lifetime investment. The American farmer looked on it as a source of get-rich-quick wealth, wanted instant gratification and was prepared to move on if his present situation dissatisfied him.

F. McLynn (2003) *Wagons West*, Pimlico, p. 22.

1. In passage 4, what historical approach is offered for US expansion west?

2. How will that approach affect the history that is written under its influence?

3. Does it have any particular limitations?

One over-arching explanation is that of 'Manifest Destiny', but even here there is disagreement as to what exactly the concept of Manifest Destiny meant. This is demonstrated in the following two passages and source B.

Passage ⑤ Manifest Destiny (1)

[Manifest Destiny] was a peculiar mixture of assertiveness and fear, of ideology and crude political calculation. Economic motives do not seem to have played a primary role. Ideologically, Manifest Destiny can be seen as a weird mixture of evangelical Protestantism, **ultramontane republicanism** *and Hegelian philosophy. History, as in Hegel's system, had a purpose of destiny and Providence had obviously chosen the United States as its vessel. Since the white race was self-evidently superior only the lily-livered would draw back from fulfilling the obvious design of the transcendent order, whether this is called God, Spirit or Providence. There had always been a strand in US Republican thought that has emphasised continual expansion as the only way to preserve the peculiar virtue of Republicanism.*

But Manifest Destiny was not a product of pure ideology. Some historians see fear of foreign nations and especially of Britain as the real impulse towards expansion. British meddling in California and Texas was particularly resented. Alongside this was a desire for expansion by the southern slave-owning states, fearful that the balance of power was swinging away from them. The incorporation of slave owning Texas would be a powerful brake on the ambitions of the abolitionists. Even those who wavered were won round by scare stories about British desire to abolish slavery world wide.

In subtle ways Manifest Destiny was important as an ideological support for pioneers who struck west in their wagons in the 1840s. Just as the Boers and the Mormons trekked into the wilderness with the conviction that God was on their side so the emigrants could feel they were caught up in a moment of inevitability, that they were History's winners. Racial prejudice and a feeling of cultural superiority were important aspects of this.

F. McLynn (2003), pp. 9–10.

Ultramontane republicanism

A political creed that favoured continuing expansion across the mountains (ultra montane), i.e. the Appalachians, to maintain their political initiative.

In what ways do passages 5 or 6 suggest different interpretations of the move west.

Passage ⑥ Manifest Destiny (2)

The Morning News was one of the dozens of cheap newspapers that revolutionised the dissemination of information in the 1830s. Its editor John L O'Sullivan coined one of the most famous phrases in American History when he insisted on 'our manifest destiny to overspread the continent'.

Manifest Destiny was not, as historians so often imply, a deeply held American folk belief. Rather it was the self-conscious creation of political propagandists like O'Sullivan determined to uncouple the politics of expansion from the growing sectional controversy over slavery.

R. V. Hine and J. M. Faragher (2000) *The American West: A New Interpretive History,* Yale University Press, pp. 199–200.

LINK UP

Intentionalist interpretations – see Chapter 1, p. 11.

In a sense, these two definitions might be termed structuralist and intentionalist. The first in passage 5 suggests that it was the institutions of the USA itself that generated the will to move west, a drive stemming from factors like the way in which the government of the USA had emerged from conflict with the British in the War of Independence or the influence of the slave culture that dominated the southern states and, from as early as the 1820s, was a growing cause of division between the states of the Union. The second definition in passage 6 focuses more on the role of individuals like O'Sullivan, who used the press to promote a particular image and objective. His famous claim that it was the USA's destiny 'to possess the whole continent' was typical of a particular attitude which has been seen as part of the 'unique American culture' referred to above.

Source (**B**) **Manifest Destiny (3)**

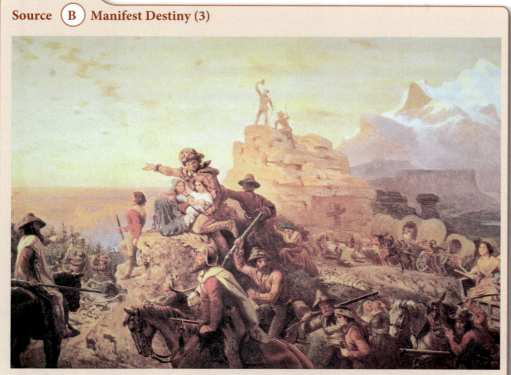

'Westward the course of Empire takes its way', a mural painting by Emanuel Gottlieb Leutze, 1861, for the US Capitol in Washington DC

Painted as a romantic image of the pioneering spirit when the westward surge was reaching new heights – possibly because of families seeking to escape the hardships and conflict of the Civil War – the painting includes such stereotypical images as frontiersmen shouldering their rifles, a pioneer bride, a dead loved one being buried by a grieving family and the ubiquitous covered wagon. At the peak of the hill is early pioneer Daniel Boone pointing the way west to a mother lying holding her child in her arms. The whole painting can be seen as an allegory of Republican plans for the post-war West.

> What does Leutze's interpretation add to our understanding of the West?

The issue of the shifting frontier is highlighted by the US government's changing policy towards the Native American Indians.

> ## Source (C) The Buffalo Creek Treaty, 1838
>
> *Whereas, the six nations of the New York Indians not long after the close of the war of the Revolution became convinced from the rapid increase of white Settlements around, that the time was not far distant when their true interest must lead them to seek a new home among their … brethren in the west … And they therefore applied to the President to take their Green Bay lands, and provide them a new home among their brethren [in the West]. And the President, being anxious to promote the peace, prosperity and happiness of his red children … the following articles of a treaty are entered into between the United States of America and the several tribes of the New York Indians …*
>
> *Article 1 The several tribes of New York Indians … hereby cede and relinquish to the United States all their right title and interest to the lands secured to them at Green Bay by the Menomonie Treaty of 1831 …*
>
> *Article 2 … the United States agree to set apart the following tract of country, situated directly west of the state of Missouri, as a permanent home … Beginning on the west line of the State of Missouri at the northeast corner of the Cherokee tract, and running thence north along the west line of the State of Missouri twenty-seven miles … to include 1,824,000 acres of land, being 320 acres for each soul of said Indians as their numbers are at present computed …*
>
> *Article 4 Perpetual peace and friendship shall exist between the United States and the New York Indians; and the United States hereby guarantee to protect and defend them in the peaceable possession and enjoyment of their new homes … The Lands secured to them … under this treaty shall never be included in any State or Territory of this Union.*
>
> Treaty with the New York Indians, Buffalo Creek, New York, 15 January 1838, in 'From Revolution to Reconstruction', Department of Alfa-Informatica, University of Groningen.

LINK UP

'From above' and 'from below' interpretations – see Chapter 1, p. 17.

The treaty signed with the New York Indian Tribes at Buffalo Creek on 15 January 1838 shows how the situation had already begun to change from a policy of living alongside to a policy of removal, though of course that is not how the Treaty puts it. This was a policy repeated up and down the eastern seaboard, and one which gradually moved west as the white population began to realise the potential of what lay beyond the eastern mountain ranges (although the central area of the Plains still continued to be labelled 'the Great American Desert' until well into the nineteenth century). By 1840, the attitude of the United States government towards the permanent 'Indian Frontier' and the lands beyond the Mississippi had undergone substantial change, and bitter experience was already beginning to suggest that there was little the Native American Indians could do about this. Even adopting US legal and political systems was not sufficient to shield them from the demands of white settlers, speculators and miners. In a very real sense, it is possible to see the whole move westwards as a move sponsored by the government directly or indirectly. That is not to say that the government adopted a specific policy of expansion nor that it was always the driving force behind the westward move, but the mechanics of establishing the US presence in the West was a political process, driven by the government.

This top-down approach can be traced also in the issue of relations with the British and their colonial expansion in Canada. It was partly an inherent distrust of the British that prompted the first major breach of the Mississippi frontier after 1840. The British threat in the North West became a major concern for the more Anglophobe element of the US political system by the 1840s. In the Oregon Treaty of 1818, 49° North (the 49th parallel) had been fixed as the boundary between the USA and the British Canadian possessions, while to the west the Oregon territory was to be jointly controlled for 10 years, an arrangement extended indefinitely in 1827.

The Oregon territory stretched from the border of California (42° North) to Russia's Alaska territory (54°40′ North). In 1844, the new president James K. Polk was elected on a slogan of 'fifty-four forty or fight'. Such a demand for the whole Pacific coast of the continent was clearly not acceptable to the British/Canadian government and, in practice, the USA was ready to accept the continuation of the 49th parallel to the Pacific, but it produced serious political disputes in the USA. In 1841, Senator Linn of Missouri introduced a bill to grant free land to any settler prepared to travel the difficult overland trail to Oregon, thereby seeking to increase settlement and enhance the USA's claim to Oregon. He was opposed by southern senators, who saw this as a direct assault on the British, and who depended heavily on trade with Britain for the support of their cotton and tobacco plantations. Linn's response can be seen in source D.

Source D The value of Oregon

The Senator from South Carolina somewhat inconsistently urges that the country is bleak, barren, volcanic, rocky, a waste, always flooded when it is not parched; and insists that, worthless as it is, Great Britain will go at once to war for it. Strange that she should in 1818 have held so tenaciously to what is worthless! Stranger still that she should have stuck yet closer to it in 1827 when she had still ample time to discover the worthlessness of the possession! And strangest of all that she should still cling to it with the grasp of death! Sir, I cannot help but think that she and the Senator have formed a very different estimate of the territory and that she (Great Britain) is, as she ought to be, a good deal better informed.

Senator Linn's address to the Senate, quoted in F. McLynn (2003), p. 24.

> How might sources C and D be used to support alternative interpretations of the West?

The issue was finally settled in the Treaty of 1846 at some cost to Canada, which lost fertile land to which it had a prior claim, but more importantly the whole dispute led to the opening of the Oregon Trail and a steady stream of wagons westwards.

There are other factors that played their part in the westward expansion, not least the rush to find gold or other precious minerals in the hills and mountains of the West. There is also the suggestion that the West served as a safety valve for the industrial development of the East, providing an outlet for goods and a destination for surplus populations. Horace Greeley, editor of the *New York Weekly Tribune*, wrote that 'every smoke that rises in the Great West marks a new customer to the counting rooms and warehouses of New York'. The Civil War also undoubtedly played a part in pushing people westward, but underlying all of these remains the question of individual motivation versus collective cultural imperative.

Stretch and challenge

Are alternative interpretations necessarily conflicting interpretations?

Passage 7 Expansion

With the acquisition of Oregon, Texas and California and the new Southwest, the United States became a transcontinental nation. The unorganised territory of the trans-Mississippi West constituted 49 percent of the country's land. In this vast region the federal government would assume unprecedented authority over the next forty years. The native peoples of the West would be conquered by federal armies, the land surveyed by federal engineers and the territories administered by federal bureaucrats, as historian Richard White argues, by exercising its power in the West the federal government greatly expanded its own authority. In the American political system states and localities exercised countervailing power with the national government. But the Indian and Mexican communities of the West were targets for federal conquest and colonisation – disempowerment.

Passage **continued**

One of the first steps in this process was the creation by Congress in 1849 of the Department of the Interior, consolidating in one government agency the Bureau of Indian Affairs and the General Land Office and soon adding the Geological Survey and the Territorial Office. The Federal department charged with protecting the Indians' rights to their lands thus also became responsible for assessing the value of and dividing up the national domain, distributing it to settlers and creating new territories and states. That this did not strike Americans as an absurd contradiction speaks volumes about the attitude of the government on the eve of the violent period of disempowerment that was beginning.

The designation of the Great Plains as Indian Country in perpetuity had been essential to the logic of the 'Indian Removal'. But the new geopolitical reality of continentalism invalidated this premise. Already officials were seriously discussing possible routes for a transcontinental railroad and thousands of Americans were travelling across the plains on the overland trails to the Pacific. Although few Americans were, as yet, settling in the Plains themselves, emigrants were consuming timber from the river bottoms for their campfires, grazing their livestock on the crops of native farmers and hunting antelope and buffalo by the thousands …

R. V. Hine and J. M. Faragher (2000), pp. 216–7.

In all of this, it was the Native American Indians whose way of life was progressively undermined and ultimately destroyed.

Passage **The fate of the Plains Indians**

The true history of the American Indians is only just being written and unfortunately it has until now been largely in the hands of enthusiasts who have allowed their sympathies to cloud the objective truth. The Indians were not murderous savages … Nor were they the sophisticated primitive innocents living in utopian and preservationist communities brutally disturbed by cruel and heedless invaders … Mining interests were particularly ruthless in evading treaties and then bribing or persuading authorities into sanctioning breaches.

There was no lack of sympathy on the white side. Helen Hunt Johnson (1830–85) produced a carefully documented history of breaches of Indian treaties called A Century of Dishonour *which shocked the authorities into action. Her book led Senator Henry L Dawes to put through … the Dawes Act (1887) to turn the nomadic plains Indians, who seemed doomed, into settled farmers by allotting each head of family a quarter section. These lands were inalienable and were held in federal trust for 25 years. This act was criticised for opening up the Indian reserve lands to whites … but this ignores the fact that many Indians took advantage of it and thus got full citizenship, did not sell their lands after 25 years and became full members of the American farming community.*

P. Johnson (1997) *A History of the American People,* Weidenfeld and Nicholson, p. 531.

With the closing of the frontier, it may have seemed that the Indian question had also been closed, but an examination of the Native American Indian perspective shows that this was not entirely the case. Studies of the West from the Native American point of view might suggest that it was the policy that sought to destroy their way of life and cultural identity which in the end helped to save it. One of the problems the Native

American Indians always had was that each tribe had its own version of the Indian language, culture and religion – its own tribal identity – which it sought to defend against other tribes. Being forced to learn English ironically gave them a common understanding of their own language and the idea of an overall Indian lingua franca developed which led to the rise of a pan-Native American Indian religion in the second decade of the twentieth century.

Passage 9 An Indian response

In the 1920s, Antonio Luhan, a Taos Pueblo Indian, showed John Collier the poor living conditions in American Indian communities. In response, Collier formed the American Indian Defense Association. For the next decade, Collier headed Indian reform efforts. In 1933, President Roosevelt appointed him commissioner of Indian affairs.

American Indian culture had been stripped away by measures like the Dawes Act which had ended tribal government and authorised the sale of tribal lands. Between 1887 and 1934, the government took over 90 million acres of tribal lands previously guaranteed by treaties and federal law. Dawes is quoted as saying that to be civilised one must 'wear civilised clothes ... cultivate the ground, live in houses, ride in Studebaker wagons, send children to school ...'. Collier worked to get the Indian Reorganization Act of 1934 passed which reversed the Dawes Act policy.

Adapted from American Indian Defense Association.

Passages 8 and 9 give two different views of the Dawes Act.

1. How do these reflect different approaches to the history of the Plains Indians?

2. Examine the advantages and disadvantages of using one of these approaches to consider the issue of the fate of the Plains Indians.

The Native American Indians were the victims of progressive changes in policy from the early settlers, who sought to live alongside them and learn how to make the best use of the lands that they were discovering. Succeeded by the idea of removing the American Indians to lands that were unlikely to appeal to white settlers only delayed the further onset of difficulties. However, the idea of an ongoing battle between white and Native Americans that reduces the West to a state of almost constant warfare and bloodshed is equally unrealistic. Films of the American West from the 1930s to the 1960s painted an almost unremittingly negative image of the Native American. At the same time, the revival of a sense of Indian community continued, and the Civil Rights movement in the 1950s and 1960s encouraged the growth of a similar movement for Native American Rights.

Conclusion

Ultimately, there are as many American Wests as there are cultural groups making up the national community. From the Native American Indians, who first settled the prairies, to the Asian settlers, who left their homeland after the failure of the American War in Vietnam, the USA has constantly sought to assimilate new cultures, and in a sense, the 'Frontier' is still a formative feature of the American character.

THINK LIKE AN HISTORIAN

Re-read the case study about the US expansion west, and work through the two questions that follow.

(a) What can you learn from passage 7 about the interpretations, approaches and methods of this historian? Refer to the extract and your knowledge to explain your answer.

EXAM TIP

When answering question (a), you will need to do *two* things:

(i) Support your answer by *detailed* reference to the extract AND refer to alternative approaches/methods.

(ii) Use relevant and accurate knowledge as part of a thorough analysis of the interpretation.

(b) The concept of Manifest Destiny has sometimes been used to explain the US expansion westwards in the nineteenth century. In what ways can the usefulness of this concept be demonstrated? What are the strengths and weaknesses of this as the basis for an approach to studying the development of the West?

EXAM TIP

As with (a) questions, you will have to do *two* things to achieve a top grade in (b) questions:

(i) Show both advantages and disadvantages/shortcomings of the approach/method, AND compare it with other approaches/methods.

(ii) Use relevant and accurate knowledge to assess both advantages *and* disadvantages.

EXAM TIP

Before submitting your answer to the questions above and moving on to the next case study, use the checklist on page 92 to make sure you have taken the right approach for a top grade.

Stretch and challenge

In recent years, Native American tribes have successfully challenged the US government over nineteenth-century policies towards their lands and have received millions of dollars in compensation. How does this reflect on different interpretations of the US expansion in Native American lands?

Case study 4: Debates about the Holocaust

Introduction

Few issues in history have raised such a widespread emotional response as the Holocaust. The investigation of responsibility since the end of the Second World War in 1945 and the opening up of the camps to demonstrate the full horrors of the Nazis' treatment of the Jewish population of Europe between 1933 and 1945 has led to discussion and disputes over the responsibility of everyone involved, from placing the entire blame on Hitler to the inference that the leaders of the Jewish populations were themselves in some way complicit in the fate of their own people.

Disagreements over the different aspects of the Holocaust have developed over the years. In the immediate post-war period, there was reluctance on all sides to discuss it. Substantial historical research into the Holocaust only really began in the 1960s, and was sparked by the highly publicised trial of **Adolf Eichmann** in Jerusalem in 1961. This growing interest also led to a rapid growth of indiscriminate publication of popular literature about the Holocaust, often with little basis in serious academic research. Along with this came some extreme interpretations of what happened to the Jews in Germany and eastern Europe between 1933 and 1945.

> ### BIOGRAPHY
>
> **Adolf Eichmann**, senior SS officer and head of the Department for Jewish Affairs in the Gestapo 1941–5, has been as described as 'the architect of the Holocaust'. Eichmann escaped from Germany in 1945 and fled to Argentina. He was eventually tracked down and kidnapped by the Israeli secret police. In 1961, he was put on trial in Israel for crimes against humanity. He was found guilty and executed in 1962.

Studies focused on Nazi leadership, especially the role of Hitler.

> ### Passage (1) Hitler's antisemitism
>
> *… some time in his early life Hitler became a violent anti-Semite. His hatred of the Jews became stronger with every passing day and remained with him for the rest of his life. The day before he committed suicide he pledged his successors to observe 'the scrupulous observation of the racial laws and … an implacable opposition against the universal poisoner of all peoples, international Jewry'. Hitler saw the Jews as constituting not a religious group, but a scheming and unscrupulous race whose members sought to weaken superior races by defiling and polluting their blood. He believed he had a divine mission to combat the Jewish menace.*
>
> *Hitler's ideological beliefs developed over time and he had no pre-arranged idea of how he would put them into practice. But they lay at the heart of his plans for the development of Germany after 1933 and gave coherence to the process of decision making in Nazi Germany.*
>
> C. Culpin and R. Henig (1997) *Modern Europe 1870–1945*, Longman, pp. 290–1.

More recently, Daniel Goldhagen has shifted and broadened that focus, looking predominantly on an area of responsibility that he sees as long neglected by other historical studies. He reaches very clear conclusions, but he also acknowledges that other factors might have had a part to play.

Passage 2 Goldhagen's interpretation

For what developments would a comprehensive explanation of the Holocaust have to account? For the extermination of the Jews to occur four principle things were necessary:

- *The Nazis – that is the leadership, specifically Hitler – had to decide to undertake the extermination.*

- *They had to gain control over the Jews, namely over the territory in which they resided.*

- *They had to organise the extermination and devote to it sufficient resources.*

- *They had to induce a large number of people to carry out the killings.*

The vast literature on Nazism and the Holocaust, treats in great depth the first three elements as well as others such as the origins and character of Hitler's genocidal beliefs and the Nazis' ascendancy to power, yet as I have already indicated it has treated the last element … perfunctorily and mainly by assumption. It is therefore essential to discuss here some analytical and interpretative issues that are central to studying the perpetrators.

Until recently virtually no research had been done … save on the leaders of the Nazi regime. In the last few years some publications have appeared that treat one group or another, yet the state of our knowledge about the perpetrators remains deficient. We know little about many of the institutions of killing, little about many aspects of the perpetration of the genocide and still less about the perpetrators themselves. As a result popular and scholarly misconceptions abound including the following.

It is commonly believed that the Germans slaughtered Jews by and large in the gas chambers and that without gas chambers, modern means of transportation and efficient bureaucracies, the Germans would have been unable to kill millions of Jews. The belief persists that somehow only technology made horror on this scale possible.

It is generally believed by scholars and non-scholars alike that the perpetrators were primarily, overwhelmingly, SS men, the most devoted and brutal Nazis.

It has been an unquestioned truism that had a German refused to kill a Jew, then he himself would have been killed, sent to a concentration camp or severely punished.

All these views…. held unquestioningly as … self-evident truths … have distorted the way in which this period is understood

D. Goldhagen (1996) *Hitler's Willing Executioners: Ordinary Germans and the Holocaust*, Little, Brown Book Group.

Try to identify key words and phrases that might help you to classify the approach which is being taken by Goldhagen.

Goldhagen then seeks to focus attention on 'ordinary Germans' rather than on systems and structures or individuals and intentions.

Intentionalist historians such as Lucy Davidowitz point to Hitler's obsessive anti-Semitism as a basis for the argument that Hitler conceived the idea of exterminating the Jews as early as the 1920s, citing the views expressed in *Mein Kampf* to support this idea. They suggest that through his domestic and foreign policies the idea of extermination was remorselessly pursued from the moment Hitler came to power in 1933. Based on this argument, it is possible, with hindsight, to trace the measures against the Jews in a way that suggests there was a deliberate and planned escalation from the Nuremburg Laws (1935) through Kristallnacht (1938) to the ghettoisation of the eastern European Jews and eventually their forced removal to the camps and the introduction of the Final Solution under cover of all-out war.

LINK UP

Intentionalist interpretations – see Chapter 1, p. 11.

Structuralist interpretations – see Chapter 1, p. 12.

Structuralist historians (functionalists), however, do not see such an obvious process of development. Writers like Hans Mommsen and Martin Broszat suggest that Hitler drifted into the Holocaust as a result of the competitive conflict between his subordinates to raise their own profile (and thus their power in the Nazi system). The adoption of the Final Solution was just a part of this struggle by the Nazi magnates to advance their own interests by pleasing Hitler. Supporters of this view point to the early Nazi policy of allowing the Jewish population to flee – by 1940, more than half the Jewish populations of Germany and Austria had left those countries – and suggest that it was the outbreak of the war that produced a new policy. The push to the east to win *Lebensraum* and the consequent rapid growth in the Jewish population under German rule resulting from conquests in Poland, and later western Russia and the other eastern territories, created a situation that could not be dealt with by the methods employed so far, leading to more devastating solutions.

> **Passage** **Cumulative radicalisation**
>
> *The notion that the Nazis proceeded incrementally against the Jews goes against the understandable desire to point to a single moment when one crucial decision was made, but history is not so easily resolved. The decisions that led to a killing technique that delivered families to their deaths by a railway link that stopped metres from the crematoria took years to evolve. The Nazi regime was one that practised 'cumulative radicalisation' whereby each decision often led to a crisis that led to a still more radical decision ... All the leading Nazis knew that their Fuhrer prized one quality in decision making above all others: radicalism.*
>
> L. Rees (2005) *Auschwitz – the Nazis and the Final Solution,* BBC Books, pp. 16–7.

How might the idea of 'cumulative radicalism' contribute to a specific approach to the issue of the Holocaust?

Goldhagen acknowledges all of this but suggests that none of this is critical; that without the active involvement or at least passive acquiescence of the German public neither Hitler's intentions nor the structure of the Nazi state could have orchestrated the attempted destruction of an entire racial group.

In 1963, Hannah Arendt even suggested that the Jews themselves were in some way complicit in their own destruction.

> **Passage** **Jewish responsibility**
>
> *In 1963 the Jewish scholar Hannah Arendt claimed that 'if the Jewish people had really been unorganised and leaderless there would have been chaos and plenty of misery but the total number of victims would hardly have been between four and a half and six million people'. Arendt charged Jewish leaders with helping the process of destruction by complying with Nazi orders to supply names and groups of Jews for transportation to the death camps.*
>
> A. Farmer (1998) *Anti-Semitism and the Holocaust,* Hodder Murray, pp. 8–9.

Goldhagen's views were challenged by Christopher Browning in his study of *Ordinary Men* (1998). In his investigation of a single police unit, Browning argued that the consequences of their situation – the effects of the war and Nazi propaganda, the indoctrination that many had received through their education under the Nazi system and time in the Hitler Youth, and the simple effects of peer pressure to conform – led ordinary men to behave with extraordinary cruelty. He identified German racial imperialism as being responsible for the Final Solution, and while antisemitism was the

extreme reflection of this, there was a general acceptance of the need to slaughter thousands of Poles and Soviets which made it possible to move on to the idea of the destruction of *all* European Jews, an idea that was simply accepted as another facet of the mass murders already being committed by 'ordinary' Germans.

Passage **5   The Wannsee Conference**

On January 20th 1942, 15 high-ranking Nazi Party and German government officials gathered at a villa in the Berlin suburb of Wannsee to discuss and co-ordinate the implementation of the Final Solution. Invitees did not deliberate whether such a plan (the Final Solution) should be undertaken, but instead discussed the realisation of a decision that had already been made … None of the officials present objected to the policy announced by Heydrich.

Heydrich indicated that approximately 11,000,000 Jews were eventually to be subjected to the 'Final Solution' … Despite the euphemisms that appeared in the protocols of the meeting the aim of the Wannsee Conference was clear: the co-ordination of a policy of genocide of European Jews.

United States Holocaust Memorial Museum, 'Wannsee Conference and the "Final Solution"', *Holocaust Encyclopedia..*

The Wannsee Conference confirmed a process already begun. It involved not only the Nazi leadership but also wide swathes of government departments in the procedures for the collection, transportation and destruction of vast numbers of men, women and children and, as such, it is difficult to see how it can be claimed that ordinary Germans knew little about what was going on.

Source **A   Individual perspectives of Nazi action**

'I don't blame people who didn't come forward, but to say they didn't know what was going on is rubbish: in school, in university you knew not exactly what happened, but that Jews disappeared. We thought the worst because my husband said "If they were still alive we would hear from them" but the fact was they had disappeared, they were just not there. That, I think, for my family and friends who were against Hitler, was the greatest encouragement to resist: that citizens can just disappear. As my father said: "Germany was a country without law."'

Inga Haag, member of the anti-Hitler resistance, in L. Smith (2006) *Forgotten Voices of the Holocaust*, Random House, p. 304.

'I have to say that my father began to have doubts (about the Party) when the Jews were deported and also when the handicapped people disappeared. One day my Grandmother came back from Breslau and told my father "Konrad, I was standing on the platform when a very long train arrived with many women and children in it. There was a woman who called from the train window "dear lady please bring me a glass of water". Well grandmother went and got water from a water pipe which had paper cups and then brought it to the woman and then an SS officer who was patrolling backwards and forwards next to the train knocked the water out of her hand and said "watch it those are Jews".'

A child from Strehlen, Germany, quoted in Smith (2006), pp. 86–7.

In a small group, discuss the following:

1. How reliable do you think the observations of the people in source A might be?

2. Consider the problems that historians might have in finding reliable sources. What factors might have influenced records made in the period of Nazi rule?

3. In what way might such difficulties affect our analysis of the responsibility of the German people for the Holocaust?

4. What type of approach to the issue of the Holocaust might find source A useful? What sort of problems might be involved in such an approach?

Does this support the idea that the German people were aware of the Holocaust, or are a small number of individual recollections insufficient to make general judgements? Goldhagen would argue that knowledge was widespread and that even if there was a lack of knowledge of the actual process, there was an implicit understanding that something was being done to the Jews. From this, he would infer that the German population as a whole shared some of the guilt for the fate of the Jews; that they were complicit in the Final Solution even if they were not directly implicated. However, some police reports would seem to undermine this suggestion, for example the **RSHA** issued the following decree in October 1941.

Passage (6) German-Jewish fraternisation

Recently it has been repeatedly noticed here that, as in the past people of German blood maintain friendly relations to Jews and blatantly show themselves with Jews in public. As these people of German blood in question even today display total incomprehension regarding the most elementary principles of National Socialism and their behaviour may be seen as contemptuous of official policy, I order that on such occasions the person of German blood is to be taken into temporary custody on educational grounds. The Jews in each case to be arrested for incarceration in a concentration camp.

RSHA Decree, 24 October 1941, quoted in C. Browning (2005) *The Origins of the Final Solution*, Arrow Books, p. 390.

QUICK FACT

The **Reich Security Main Office (RSHA)** was formed in 1939 under Reinhard Heydrich. Its departments included the Gestapo and SS intelligence agency (the SD).

Source B shows the distribution of concentration camps and death camps across the Third Reich. Consider how the map might be used to support alternative theories. Structuralists, for example, might use it to support the idea that the Final Solution was a response to the eastward expansion and changing situation after the outbreak of war in 1939 since the extermination camps are predominantly in conquered territories, thus suggesting a developing policy. The distance of such camps from the heartland of Germany might also be used by those seeking to limit the amount of blame that could be placed on ordinary Germany as most Jews were from the conquered territories and distant from the thoughts or interests of ordinary Germans.

Source (B) The geography of the Holocaust

The distribution of concentration camps and death camps across the Third Reich

The willingness of individuals to carry out Nazi policies cannot be without significance, but as Goldhagen pointed out above, other historians have suggested that the blame for the Holocaust lies with other psychological features of the German population.

How might sources B and C be useful in supporting or undermining a specific approach to the debate over the Holocaust?

Source C Anti-Jewish campaign in a Bavarian village

The banner says 'Jews are not welcome here'

Passage 7 German antisemitism

One of the main reasons for Hitler's rise to power was that large numbers of Germans had some sympathy with his views.

Most right-wing parties after 1918 were anti-Semitic. Virtually every major German institution – the army, civil service, judiciary, churches – was also permeated by anti-Semitism. Many Germans, young and old alike, declared openly and proudly that they were anti-Semitic. Some continued to believe in The Protocols of the Elders of Zion *[first published in Russia in 1903], which purported to be a record of a secret meeting at which leading Jews plotted world domination, though this was exposed as a clumsy Russian forgery in 1921.*

In the early 1930s it does seem that large numbers of people of every class, age, region or gender accepted the Nazi anti-Semitic message either fully or in part. Not all Germans were violently anti-Semitic: few believed that Hitler would 'eliminate' all Germany's Jews. But most expected – and many hoped – that Hitler would take some action against the Jews.

A. Farmer (1998), pp. 18–9.

It is important to consider to what extent such an underlying feeling might have been exploited by propaganda.

Source **Antisemitic poster for the Nazi propaganda film,** *Der Ewige Jude*

'Der Ewige Jude' *(the Eternal Jew) was a Nazi propaganda film made on the orders of Joseph Goebbels, the minister in charge of Nazi propaganda, in 1939–40, shortly after the invasion of Poland. It was in the form of a documentary, contrasting antisemitic images of the Jews with the ideal life of the Nazi state. This poster is for a Dutch version shown in Nazi-occupied Holland.*

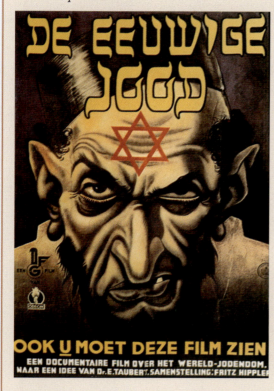

Historians such as Browning and Goldhagen have largely examined the same documents and archives, but the difference lies in their approach. While Browning has emphasised the structural pressures to conform, Goldhagen's perspective is based on an explicit interest in:

> '… ideas and mindsets that lead to people's actions: not structural causes, but what he calls "ideational causes of social action". Although he acknowledges that the incentive structure is important he believes that this alone cannot cause people to act, but works "in conjunction with the cognitive and value structures" already in place in the individual.' (R. Eaglestone (2001) *Postmodernism and the Holocaust*, p. 32)

Conclusion

Ultimately, even given the same information different perspectives will lead to different emphases and variations in conclusions, and it is difficult to see how far the questions of the role of ordinary Germans can ever be fully explained by simply applying one approach to the issues involved. History will always require judgements based on the evidence. It is this which leaves an opening for those who would deny the Holocaust, claiming that the death of 6 million Jews did not happen. The legal judgement against the most well-known **Holocaust denier, David Irving**, in 2000, suggests that such claims are simply not history. Judge The Hon. Mr Justice Gray concluded:

QUICK FACT

Holocaust denier David Irving claimed that he had been libelled by the American historian, Deborah Lipstadt in her book *Denying the Holocaust: The Assault on Truth and Memory* (Penguin, 1994), in which she attacked Irving's assertions about the Holocaust. When the libel case went to court, the judge found in favour of the defendants, Penguin Books and Deborah Lipstadt.

'… the charges which I have found to be substantially true include the charge that Irving has for his own ideological reasons persistently and deliberately misrepresented and manipulated historical evidence; that for the same reasons he has portrayed Hitler in an unwarrantedly favourable light, principally in relation to his attitude towards and responsibility for the treatment of the Jews.' (Judgement 13.167, quoted in Eaglestone (2001), p. 3.

THINK LIKE AN HISTORIAN

Re-read the case study about responsibility for the Holocaust, and work through the questions that follow:

(a) What can you learn from passage 2 about the interpretations, approaches and methods of this historian? Refer to the extract and your knowledge to explain your answer.

EXAM TIP

When answering question (a), you will need to do *two* things:

(i) Support your answer by *detailed* reference to the extract AND refer to alternative approaches/methods.

(ii) Use relevant and accurate knowledge as part of a thorough analysis of the interpretation.

(b) Some historians have focused on the idea of 'Hitler's willing executioners' in explaining how the Holocaust was possible. Explain how this has contributed to our understanding of the Holocaust. Has this approach any disadvantages or shortcomings?

EXAM TIP

As with (a) questions, you will have to do *two* things to achieve a top grade in (b) questions:

(i) Show both advantages and disadvantages/shortcomings of the approach/method, AND compare it with other approaches/methods.

(ii) Use relevant and accurate knowledge to assess both advantages *and* disadvantages.

EXAM TIP

Before submitting your answer to the questions above, use the checklist on page 92 to make sure you have taken the right approach for a top grade.

Stretch and challenge

Using the passages and sources in the above case study and your wider knowledge, consider how valid is the argument that some interpretations of the Holocaust are simply not history. Use relevant examples to support your answer.

Exam Café
Relax, refresh, result!

Relax and prepare

What I wish I had known at the start of the year …

Bhavesh

I found it helpful to make a list of the different approaches to the topic, and then write notes about several examples that support the explanation and some that seem to disprove it. Once I had done this for each approach, I was able to compare them and see their different strengths and weaknesses.

Dean

At first, I didn't understand why we had to try to remember all the different views of what was happening. I thought it was enough just to describe it. Then my teacher likened it to a football match where the fans of the winning team described the game differently from the fans whose team had lost. There are other views too – the football commentator is likely to have a different view from the match referee. Now, I realise that there can be several different interpretations of the same historical event. From this, all I have to do is explain why such different conclusions can be drawn!

Susie

To start with, I lost marks because I didn't point out both the advantages and disadvantages of the interpretation.

Eva

My marks improved as soon as I made sure that I supported whatever I said with examples from my own knowledge.

First, you have to be able to recognise different interpretations of past events; that is the starting point, but it goes much further than that.

The next thing is to explain how each of those interpretations might have been arrived at. You will need to recognise that there are different ways of interpreting the same set of events, or that someone might have a very different point of view because the criteria they are using to judge the situation are very different.

There may be different ways of approaching any question you are asked, but the important thing is that whatever arguments you produce must be supported by using examples from your own knowledge. This means that you have to have read about different ideas for yourself and be able to explain how they connect to the events.

You will need to be able to show why different interpretations might have certain advantages, but also be able to analyse their disadvantages.

Refresh your memory

Revision checklist:

Make sure that you are aware of different explanations of witch hunting (though all tend to relate in some way to issues of instability):

▷ as a weapon of confessional conflict

▷ as a response to disaster

▷ as a means of social control

▷ as a function of the needs of society

▷ as a reflection of rampant misogyny

▷ as a deep rooted survival of paganism

▷ as a top-down process

▷ as a bottom up process.

Question

(b) Some historians have focused on political/legal changes to explain the phenomenon of the European witch craze in the sixteenth and early seventeenth centuries. Explain how this can contribute to our understanding of the issue? What are the advantages and disadvantages of this approach?

Example answers

Examiner says:

Bhavesh has explained the 'top-down' theory of witch-hunts and includes examples that might be used to support the explanation. The answer could perhaps do with other examples of how top-down explanations work, and it is important that you build up a good stock of examples. It would be helpful to be familiar with the ideas of Muchembled or of Larner and Elliot and their ideas on the way in which rulers with their concern for creating a compliant population were willing to use the violent suppression of anything that was indicative of deviation in order to assert that control. There is no single vital example you need to quote. You must simply make sure you have access to a good range of examples that demonstrates the strengths and weaknesses of a particular approach.

Bhavesh's answer: question (b)

It has been argued that it was general changes in the way Europe was governed that led to the witch craze. With the break up of the Catholic church more power was concentrated in the hands of the kings and other rulers. In order for them to control their kingdoms they had to take control in the courts of matters that had previously been dealt with by the church and it is argued by writers like Levack that this led to an increase in the number of cases. He gives examples of a number of situations where rulers actually led the development of witchcraft laws and prosecutions, one of these was king James VI of Scotland (later James I of England) who was supposed to have become convinced that there was a witches' conspiracy against him and launched one of the biggest witch hunts in Scottish History. This suggests a top-down drive against witchcraft – it was the government or their local representative trying to make sure that the people they ruled knew who was in charge. This fits quite a lot of the evidence in Germany, for example all the minor rulers were keen to keep control especially when threatened by religious divisions. One of the best examples of this is the Archbishop of Augsburg who directed one of the worst examples of a witch hunt in order to impose his religious ideas on the people he ruled.

On the other hand it has been argued that in this case the main motive behind the witch trial was religious. Another big problem with this argument is that often it was the local communities themselves who started the accusations with some people in a community deciding to 'sort out' their problems with other members of the community by accusing them of witchcraft. It was very easy to begin rumours about witchcraft amongst people who were basically still very superstitious. If someone argued with their neighbour and then went off muttering and a few days later some unfortunate incident occurred like a child becoming ill or an animal dying, that could start claims of witchcraft.

Levack points out that another change in state powers enabled them to use torture to get 'the truth' out of the accused. Some sorts of torture, especially the strapado were very difficult to resist and an accused witch would often quite happily accuse other neighbours of being involved and before long the whole community was divided by fear and superstition. Though the use of torture was controlled by the state the accusations often came from below and could affect even leaders of the community if they got out of control. This tends to dispute the top-down interpretation of the witch craze and suggests that it could also be a bottom-up process. The bottom-up approach has the advantage of recognising that communities were often isolated from each other and from central authorities and thus witch crazes were a product of local rivalries and personal grievances. The use of anthropological models to develop functional explanations on the whole might be seen to account for a wider selection of specific cases of witch persecution.

There are even examples such as a case in Saxony where the local magistrate refused to apply torture even though it was demanded by the local accusers of a particularly unpopular old lady, and released the accused. In this case the state authorities took the opposite role to leading the witch hunt, in fact they worked to defuse a difficult situation and a witch hunt was avoided.

Another disadvantage then of the argument that the witch hunts were a top-down process is that in some counties the authorities were sceptical about witch accusations and tended to dismiss the wild superstitious claims of neighbours and to recognise that torture was a poor tool for getting at the truth.

Like other theories of witch hunt, the idea of top-down imposition of witch hunting laws may fit some cases, but there are plenty of other cases that it does not fit. This is why it is often best to look at several possible explanations to see how they can be used together to produce a more realistic explanation of what was going on.

Introduction

Are you feeling stressed about exams? Then be reassured, this coursework unit means there will be less exam pressure. The personal study should also be an intellectually rewarding experience. With the help of your teacher, you can select a coursework topic that you want to write about. The personal study will also teach research skills – something that you should find useful in later life, especially at university.

In this unit, you will be assessed on two elements:

- ■ Your research diary, which should be no more than 1000 words.
- ■ Your personal study, which should be no more than 3000 words.

At the very core of this unit is the concept of historical significance. It is very important that this concept is incorporated into your final coursework essay as the most important driving force for your analysis. Failure to do this will result in poor performance in the final assessment. It is also essential that you develop an appropriate question which will naturally allow you to produce a response that has the concept of historical significance at its heart.

Selecting a coursework question

Below are some pointers to enable you to turn the coursework unit into a rewarding experience.

The personal study

Choosing your topic

Choosing the right topic is perhaps the single most important factor in the success or failure of the personal study. First, select a topic; secondly, phrase your actual question *around that topic*. The topic and the question must readily access the concept of historical significance as it appears in both the specification and the mark scheme. If the topic and/or the question do not easily accommodate the concept of historical significance as a primary driver of the analysis, then both should be rejected. By using the various definitions of historical significance both in the plan of research and in the final essay, you will be able to make a judgement about why different historians have interpreted the historical process in different ways and so reached sometimes very varied judgements about significance.

It is also important to consider some practical problems before opting for a given topic and question, the most important being access to sources – either primary and/or secondary. These sources may not be available in your locality even with the support of an efficient library service and the internet. An even more important consideration, however, is the range of material available for a given topic; simply put, some historical issues have received more attention from scholars than others.

Finally, your personal study has a synoptic role to play in the assessment: it should bring together and build upon skills and understanding already acquired in previous units.

Guidelines to help you choose your topic

Ask yourself:

- ■ Am I genuinely interested in the topic?
- ■ Does the topic engage the concept of historical significance head on?
- ■ Has the topic enough source material (books, primary sources, useful websites) to make it a viable study?

- Have I already studied/am studying the topic at AS/A2 Level? If so, do not use the same topic for the personal study. However, there is no reason why a topic that is just outside the time period of the other AS/A2 units should not be selected. For example, if you studied Robespierre and the French Revolution, 1774–95 for Unit F982, then Napoleon's career after 1795 might make a good choice for the personal study. There are several significant topics not covered in Units F981–986, such as Gladstone; Disraeli; Spain, 1474–1700; Mussolini; or the Cold War, 1945–65.

When selecting your topic, developing your exact question and designing your initial plan of research, it is a good idea to liaise with your teacher.

Some suggested question stems

It is obviously impossible to suggest an entire range of specific questions given that areas of study can be drawn from the full span of recorded history. Instead, below you will find some examples of question stems that might be fleshed out with specific points of significance:

- How much of a change occurred between what went before and what came after, i.e. was the individual, event or date a turning point?
- How much continuity occurred between what went before and what came after, i.e. was the individual, event or site part of a trend?
- Does the significance of the individual, event or site seem to alter when you lengthen or shorten the time scale in which it is viewed?
- Have things happened since the individual, event or site that have affected judgements about significance?
- Have different judgements about significance been contingent upon the epoch in which those judgements have been made?
- Why have historians had different judgements about significance?

Remember to avoid asking causation type questions, for example 'How significant a factor was x in causing y?'

The concept of historical significance

Syllabus B defines the concept of historical significance in very definite terms. These appear in both the specification and the mark scheme. The concept is at the very core of the A2 units and assessment, so you will need to engage it head on to do well.

In very broad terms, historical significance works on two dimensions: first, the significance of an historical event or events, individual or individuals or ideas – all three could be interwoven to produce a good response; secondly, the nature of the development of the historical process, either across time or over time, or both. For the latter, the more technical historical terms of **synchronic** or **diachronic** are used. By examining the historical problem from these different angles, you should be able to come to an understanding of why different historians have reached such different judgements about the significance of a historical development.

A good way to approach the concept of historical significance is to think of the impact of long-term developments on the historical process, as opposed to specific short-term events. A good example of this would be a battle. At first sight, a battle – which is one of the events specified above – is an obvious event that creates a dynamic historical situation. Indeed, you might argue that a given battle changes a given historical situation. If you take this view, then the Battle of Stalingrad is the most significant event of the Second World War because it checked German expansion in the east and led inevitably to German defeat. It is easy to see why an historian might reach this

Synchronic

Across time.

Diachronic

Over time.

conclusion: battles are specific points in time and they seem significant because the situation after a battle is very often different from the situation before it. Furthermore, battles produce lots of 'noise' in the sources; they are dramatic events that draw attention. Alternatively, you might argue that Stalingrad's significance is illusory because Germany was doomed to fail on the eastern front because of the sheer size of Russia, poor logistics, a weak economy, etc. Thus, Stalingrad was the product of much larger and deeply rooted historical forces and it just appears 'significant' because of the way we perceive the historical process. In this way, events, individuals or sites can be weighed against broader historical trends and development. We can also discuss why some historians consider that individuals, events or sites have the most significance as opposed to those who see longer range trends as being the really significant drivers of history.

With regard to individuals, events or sites, it is important to view them in their historical context. An event might only be deemed important if it is viewed with hindsight: 'if only Hitler had got into art school, the Second World War would never have happened' is only a valid statement if you know that Hitler became the leader of the Third Reich. You can be sure that his rejection from the art course was not deemed significant at the point it actually happened. From this, you might come to understand that historians often attribute significance to individuals, events or sites that was never seen at the time they happened or existed. You might also consider the nature of the literature that gives these individual, events or sites their significance. Most ancient and medieval sources, for example, are from a literary tradition that sees these factors as of the utmost importance. Thus, the Greek historian Arrian (c. 86–160 CE) thought that the reason for the fall of the Persian Empire was the personality and leadership of Alexander the Great rather than, for example, the nature of the governmental structure of the Persian state (which is deemed irrelevant and never even visited in the history he wrote).

Sometimes it is easier to apply this line of research to individuals and events – monarchs and battles – than sites, but consider the size and importance of one site compared to another. Take, for example, the economy of medieval England. You might argue that London appears more significant in the development of England's economy than the hundreds of small villages that surround it. It is no wonder that you might reach this conclusion because sources on London are much easier to find. After all, it was deemed important at that time and lots of important people who where literate lived in London and wrote about it. Thus, London becomes significant because of the way the sources were written (and survive) rather than because it necessarily had some inherent importance.

Significance can also be measured by recognising at least two broad dimensions in the historical process:

- Over time as part of a process that is evolving across a series of years or centuries (the diachronic element)
- Across time within the context of a given historical period (the synchronic element).

Understanding these two dimensions often gives insight into the significance of individuals, events or sites as opposed to broad trends and developments. Neither is the 'right' way of studying history. Rather, they complement each other to produce deeper understanding.

Significance over time is how we normally study history at school. We take a given geographic region, say England, and chart historical development in a chronological manner. So we start with the Norman Conquest in 1066 and end with the victory of Henry Tudor at Bosworth in 1485. We examine trends and development and see how these are linked and influenced by what goes before. Significance is often dependent and contingent on a quite narrow series of events.

Study of significance across time is rarer. This measures significance within a broad range of contemporary developments. Let's take an example. We have decided to write our essay on the reign of King John of England (1199–1216) and we will write an assessment of the significance of him as an individual. Using the significance over time dimension, we see him as part of the Angevin line whose ability to govern effectively was contingent on developments from the arrival of the Normans in England in 1066. In this manner, we might write part of our essay on John's relationship with his barons and conclude that it was bad because after a series of strong kings like his brother Richard I or father Henry II, John was relatively ineffective (caused by this legacy from the past as well as his personality). We could also approach the issue across time and argue that across Europe in the late twelfth and early thirteen centuries government was developing to such a degree that all aristocrats were beginning to feel the pinch of centralised royal administration and, as a result, they bucked against the trend and tried to face John down. Thus, the historical significance of John as an individual might be contingent simply on which dimension we wish to give the most emphasis to. Of course, neither is 'correct', but either may have influenced a given historical interpretation of the significance of John.

As discussed above, historical significance must be at the very core of your final essay and should influence your choice of question. In particular, you must not design a question that dodges the idea of historical significance for a simple causation approach (i.e. that x was more important than y in cause z). You have already proven you can do this at AS level. Rather, your question should investigate relative significance in a far more pure form. Thus, rather than asking whether Charles I caused the English Civil War, you should ask yourself if the restoration of the English monarchy in 1660 meant that the significance of the Civil War had been limited.

A good way to apply the concept of historical significance to questions is to ask a series of sub-questions. You might discuss:

- What was the nature of the individual, event or site?
  - How usual or unusual?
  - How unexpected or expected?
  - How was it received at the time?

- How wide was the impact of the individual, event or site?
  - How many people, groups or institutions were affected?
  - Were different groups – rich or poor, men or women – affected in the same way?
  - Did the impact differ according to geographic region?
  - How wide geographically was the impact?

- What was the depth of the impact?
  - How deeply were people's beliefs or attitudes affected?
  - How powerful was the impact?
  - What kind of reaction was caused?

- What was the nature of the impact?
  - How far was it beneficial or damaging?
  - Were any benefits or damage limited to certain groups?

- Were there any other issues?
  - How representative was the individual event or site?
  - Were they, or did they, become iconic or symbolic in any way?
  - How much do they reveal about the norms and beliefs of the time?

These sub-questions should lead you to consider how and why different judgements have been made about significance by historians. Further, this can be considered at different points in the process: was an individual, event or site considered significant at the time, has it been considered significant later and has its significance changed over time?

Remember that you do not have to address all, or even most of these issues, in your study. Just use the ones that are most useful or valid for your topic.

The research diary

This is an essential part of the study and final assessment. It should not exceed 1000 words. The diary should be a developing piece of writing from the very first day that you start work on your study. It should not be something that is cobbled together at the last minute.

The research diary has a dual purpose:

- It should organise and regulate the research activity. Good historians proceed along the road of research in a systematic fashion.
- It is a running commentary of your thoughts, opinions and perspectives of the historical problem at hand.

You may start the personal study with very definite ideas about the historical significance of a particular event, especially if you have encountered the historical problem in some other course. As your research proceeds, you may change your position.

Getting started

Here are two good starting points to help you make sure you get your diary properly organised. The first is to produce a simple study plan in the form of a series of short and medium-term targets. The grid below is a suggestion as to how you might formulate this part of your research diary. Not all the 'date' headings can be completed, as much depends on how your teachers structure this unit. Some centres might aim for this unit to be completed in the autumn term of Year 13 (for entry in the January exam session); other centres might spread the work for this unit over the first two terms of the Year 13 course (for entry in the June session). You are also reminded that the research diary must be submitted for marking along with the personal study.

Guide to compiling a research diary

Step	Task	Date	Outcome
1	Liaise with your teacher to identify a suitable topic for the personal study. Refer to the beginning of this chapter for guidance on choosing a suitable topic.	Final weeks of Year 12 (summer term) after the AS exams have been completed.	Initial topic selected. You should now begin to compile your research diary. Set up the research diary on computer.
2	Phrase the question (again in conjunction with your teacher), following the guidelines suggested earlier in this chapter. Justify the question by linking it to the criteria laid down for the study. Derive from this justification a series of research questions designed to address different facets of the main question.	Final weeks of Year 12, at the end of the summer term.	The provisional question is entered in the log (i.e. research diary).

3	Identify an appropriate range of source material (primary and/or secondary, websites) and comment critically upon their content, context and usefulness to the study. Begin background reading.	Summer vacation between Years 12 and 13 GCE courses.	Research notes (authors, questions, publishers, publication dates, page references, website addresses, etc.) are carefully annotated.
4	Provisional question is either confirmed or modified. If a completely new topic is now adopted, then steps 1–3 should be repeated.	Start of Year 13 course (i.e. beginning of autumn term).	Record of Programme of Study form is completed.
5	Begin to write first draft (on word processor). Plan the conduct of the study, e.g. work out deadlines. Remember technical points. Continue research. Periodically meet with teacher to monitor progress. Compile bibliography.	This depends on the centre's own Programme of Study.	Deadlines are maintained, leading to successful completion of first draft.
6	Complete final draft, noting any necessary modifications (such as the word count).	This depends on the centre's own Programme of Study.	Both the personal study and the research diary are successfully completed.
7	Submit final pieces of work for internal marking.	This depends on the centre's own Programmes of Study. Deadline for receipt of coursework marks for the January session is 10 January. Deadline for receipt of coursework marks for June Session is 15 May.	After external moderation, hopefully a good mark!

The diary is also a good way to record the details of your research. Keep a running record of the primary and secondary sources you use during your research (author, title of publication, publisher, publication date, page reference, URL). This will help in the final write-up of your essay, the bibliography and the footnotes.

The second part of the planning part of your diary is far more interesting. You should formulate a series of sub-questions that are related to your topic of study and chosen question. For example, say you have decided to study King John and your question involves an assessment of his reign. You could create the first range of sub-questions by applying a typical 'assess a leader' format to your diary. Thus, you could assess John in simple good or bad, successful or unsuccessful terms from the perspective of economics, relations with the aristocracy, success in war, dynastic objectives, etc. You may need the help of your teacher in this initial phase of your diary as, obviously, you probably won't know much about the subject you have chosen to study at that point. As your research proceeds, you should then set yourself more complex questions to consider; for example, historian x argues that John's finances were in tatters after the reign of his brother Richard I – just how far do I accept this interpretation? Thus, the diary will create a structure for your research and make you ask questions and attempt to answer them, rather than simply gathering information.

As your research progresses

Related to the first organisational function is a second much more intellectual one. As your research progresses, you will identify different interpretations related to the historical problem at hand. You will also come to understand why and how these interpretations were arrived at and, as a result, you will be able to evaluate critically the different positions assumed by historians. In consequence, this process will probably develop if not change both your interpretation of your chosen subject and your strategy for answering the question.

You may also find you have made errors in your research plan. For example, you may have pursued a given line of argument to find that it led nowhere and so was not useful for your final write-up. You should record this in your diary and perhaps discuss alternative research strategies that may have led to a more fruitful outcome.

You should also weigh up the relative use of the different books and sources you have consulted. For example, how did I decide which books and sources to use? Thus, the diary should inform the reader of *how* and *why* you came to the conclusions reached in your final essay.

It is important that the diary is a 'live' document, with additions being made to it as a continuous process alongside the research and the writing up of the final essay. It is also important that you liaise closely with your teacher as your diary develops. Your teacher should act as a mentor helping you to develop your research and advising you on potential routes of investigation that you might look into. Discussing your diary with your teacher as you progress is an excellent way of allowing them to support and encourage your thinking and understanding.

And finally ...

Once you have finished your coursework, it's a good idea to review in your diary what you have done. You might ask, for example:

- Are there any weaknesses in my work?
- Were some of the books/sources I used more helpful than others?
- Were there any books/sources that I would have liked to use but which weren't available?
- Are their areas or issues which arose during my coursework which I should have investigated further?
- Should I have done anything differently?

The publisher and authors would like to thank the following copyright holders for the extracts from:

pp. 2, 26, 38, 39: A Green and K. Troup from: *The Houses of History* © 1999 Anna Green and Kathleen Troup. Used by permission of Manchester University Press; pp.6, 8, 15, 16, 18: *History As Practice,* 2nd Edition by L.J. Jordanova © 2006. Reproduced by permission of Hodder Arnold (Publishers) Ltd; pp. 7, 11: *Whig History and Lost Causes* by J. Black. History Review © December 1995. Used by permission; pp. 7, 12, 18, 21, 27, 35–36: *Studying History* © 2000. By Jeremy Black & Donald M. MacRaild. Used by permission of Palgrave Macmillan; p. 8: *The Practice of History* by G.R. Elton © 1969. Published by Fontana. Reproduced by permission of Wiley Blackwell Publishing; pp. 8, 9: *Rethinking History* by Keith Jenkins © 1991. Published by Routledge. Used by permission of Taylor and Francis Books Ltd; p. 9: *What is History* by E.H. Carr © 1964. Used by permission of Palgrave Macmillan; p 9: Richard Evans *'In Defense of History'* in *Studying History* © 2000. By Jeremy Black & Donald M. MacRaild. Used by permission of Palgrave Macmillan; pp. 9–10, 34, 35, 39: *The Pursuit of History* © 1984 by John Tosh. Used by permission of Pearson Education; p. 11: *Change in History* by Gilbert Pleuger. History Review © March 1992. Used by permission; pp. 12, 13, 17, 25, 27, 33, 37: *The Nature of History* 3rd Edition by Arthur Marwick © 1989. Used by permission of Palgrave Macmillan; pp. 15, 16: *The Past and The Present* by L. Stone © 1981. Published by Routledge and Kegan Paul. Used by permission of Taylor and Francis Books Ltd; pp. 17, 98: *The Witch-Hunt in Early Modern Europe* © 2006 Brian Levack. Used by permission of Pearson Education; p. 19: *Feminism and History* by K. Sayer. History Today © November 1994. Used by permission; p. 19: Joan Thirsk, quoted in: *'Oxford Companion to Local & Family History'*, edited by David Hey (1996). By permission of Oxford University Press; pp. 20, 98: *Witchcraze: A New History of the European Witch Hunts* by Anne Llewellyn Barstow Copyright © 1994 by Anne Llewellyn Barstow. Reprinted by permission of HarperCollins Publishers; p. 21: *AJP Taylor: Traitor within the Gates* by Robert Cole © 1993. Used by permission of Palgrave Macmillan; p. 22: *The Witch-Craze as holocaust: The Rise of Persecuting Societies* - found in *Witchcraft Historiography* by Jonathan Barry & Owen Davies © 2007. Used by permission of Palgrave Macmillan; p. 26: L. Stone, found in: *The Houses of History* © 1999 Anna Green and Kathleen Troup. Used by permission of Manchester University Press; pp. 29, 32: *Varieties of History* 2nd ed by F. Stern © 1988. Reproduced with permission of Palgrave Macmillan; pp.36–37: *New Cultural History and You* by A. Cazoria-Sanchez from History Review © March 2008. Used by permission; p. 40: *Witchcraft in Early Modern England* © 2001 by James Sharpe. Used by permission of Pearson Education; p. 40: Peter Burke *'New Perspectives on History Writing'* in *Studying History* © 2000. By Jeremy Black & Donald M. MacRaild. Used by permission of Palgrave Macmillan; pp. 41–42: *Postmodernism and the Study of History* by R.J. Evans. History Review © December 1998. Used by permission; pp. 45, 48: *Medieval England: 1042-1228* by Toby Purser. Reprinted by permission of Pearson Education; p. 47: *The Norman Conquest* by H.R. Loyn © 1967. Published by Hutchinson. Used by permission of Taylor and Francis Books UK; p. 48: *The Feudal Kingdom of England, 1042–1216.* © 1985 Frank Barlow. Used by permission of Pearson Education; p. 49: *From Alfred to Henry III*, by Christopher Brooke © 1965. Published by Nelson; p. 50: *England and its Rulers 1066-1271* by M.T. Clanchy, published by Fontana. Reproduced by permission of Wiley-Blackwell Publishers; p. 50: *Feudal Britain* by G.W. Barrow © 1985. Reproduced by permission of Edward Arnold (Publishers) Ltd; p. 54: *Stuart England* by J.P. Kenyon © 1985, published by Penguin; p. 55; *The Century of Revolution* by C. Hill © 1961, published by Routledge. Used by permission of Taylor and Francis Books Ltd; p. 56; L. Stone's 'The Bourgeois Revolution of Seventeenth-century England revisited' found in: *Reviving the English Revolution*. Published by Verso; p. 58: *Authority and Conflict: England, 1603-58* by Derek Hirst © 1990. Reproduced by permission of Edward Arnold (Publishers) Ltd; p. 58: *The origins of the English Civil War* by Conrad Russell © 1991. Used by permission of Palgrave Macmillan; pp. 63, 78: *Industry and Empire: From 1750 to the Present Day* by E J Hobsbawm (Penguin Books 1968, third edition 1999) Copyright © EJ Hobsbawm, 1968, 1969, 1999. Used by permission of Penguin Books and David Higham Associates; pp. 71, 72: *The Making of the Second World War* by Anthony Adamthwaite © 1977, published by Allen and Unwin. Used by permission of the author; p. 72: D. Dilks and J. Ramsden from their book: *The Conservatives: A History of Their origins to 1965* © 1977, David Dilks and John Ramsden. Published by Allen and Unwin. Used by permission of David Higham Associates; p. 73: R. Henig. Used by permission of: Sempringham Publishing (the *new perspective* journal and ehistory.org.uk); p. 73: *The Inter-War Crisis, 1919-1939* © 1994 by R J Overy. Used by permission of Pearson Education; p. 83: *A History of Europe* by H.A. L. Fisher © 1936. Reproduced by permission of Hodder Arnold (Publishers) Ltd; p. 84: *God's War* by Christopher Tyerman, Copyright © Christopher Tyerman 2006. Published by Penguin. Reproduced with permission of Curtis Brown Group Ltd, London on behalf of Christopher Tyerman; p. 85: *What Were The Crusades? 3rd Edition* by Jonathan Riley-Smith © 1975. Used by permission of Palgrave Macmillan; p. 87: *Crusade Superheroes* by Jonathan Phillips © 2007. Published by BBC History Magazine 2007. Used by permission; p. 88: *Revisiting the Crusades* by Faisal Kutty © 1999. Used by permission of the author; p. 89: Extract of: Ibn al-Qalanisi, 1160, quoted in: *Arab Historians of the Crusades* by F. Gabrieli © 1992. Published by Routledge. Used by permission of Taylor and Francis Books (UK); pp. 94, 95: *Witchcraft and Magic in Sixteenth & Seventeenth Century Europe* by G. Scarre & J. Callow © 2001. Used by permission of Palgrave Macmillan; pp. 95, 99: *Witchcraft and Judgment in Reformation Germany* by R. Scribner. History Today © April 1990. Used by permission; p. 96: *Witchcraft Sourcebook* by Brian Levack © 2004, Published by Routledge. Used by permission of Taylor and Francis Books Ltd; p. 101: *Alistair Cooke's America* by Alistair Cook © 1973, published by BBC Books. Reprinted by permission of the Estate of Alistair Cooke; pp. 102, 103, 104, 108: *The American West: A New Interpretive History* by Robert Hine and John Mack Faragher © 2000. Used by permission of Yale University Press; pp. 103, 104: *Wagons West* by FJ McLynn, published by Pimlico. Reprinted by permission of The Random House Group Ltd; p. 111: *Modern Europe 1870-1945* © 1997 by Chris Culpin, Ruth Henig and Eric Evans. Used by permission of Pearson Education; p. 112: From *Hitler's Willing Executioners* by Daniel Jonah Goldhagen, copyright © 1996 by Daniel Jonah Goldhagen; Maps copyright © 1996 by Mark Stein Studios. Used by permission of Alfred A. Knopf, a division of Random House, Inc. As well as, Little Brown Book Group Ltd; p. 113: *Auschwitz – The Nazis and the Final Solution'* by L. Rees. Used by permission of Random House UK and Perseus Books USA; pp. 113, 116: *Anti-Semitism and the Holocaust* by Alan Farmer © 1998. Used by permission of Hodder & Stoughton; p. 114: Wannsee Conference and the Final Solution', from the *Holocaust Encyclopedia*. Used by the kind permission of the United States Holocaust Memorial Museum; p. 114: *Forgotten Voices of the Holocaust*, by Lyn Smith, published by Ebury Press. Reprinted by permission of The Random House Group Ltd; p. 115: From: *'The Origins of the Final Solution: The Evolution of Nazi Jewish Policy, September 1939-March 1942'* by Christopher Browning, published by Arrow. Reprinted by permission of The Random House Group Ltd. Also published in North America by the University of Nebraska Press. (c) 2004 by Yad Vashem, the Holocaust Martyrs' and Heroes Remembrance Authority, Jerusalem, Israel; pp. 117, 118: *Postmodernism and Holocaust Denial* © 2001 Robert Eaglestone, courtesy of Icon Books, London, UK.

Every effort has been made to contact copyright holders of material reproduced in this book. Any omissions will be rectified in subsequent printings if notice is given to the publishers.

Bibliography

Chapter 1

Barry, J. and Davies, O. (eds) (2007) *Witchcraft Historiography*, Palgrave Macmillan.

Barstow, A. (1994) *Witchcraze*, Pandora.

Black, J. (1995) 'Whig history and lost causes', in *History Review*, December.

Black, J. and MacRaild, D. (2000) *Studying History*, Macmillan.

Carr, E. H. (1964) *What is History?* Penguin.

Cole, R. (1993) *A. J. P. Taylor: The Traitor Within the Gates,* Macmillan.

Elton, G. R. (1969) *The Practice of History*, Fontana.

Green, A. and Troup, K. (1999) *The Houses of History*, Manchester University Press.

Hey, D. (1996) *The Oxford Companion to Local and Family History,* Oxford University Press.

Jenkins, K. (1991) *Rethinking History*, Routledge.

Jordanova, L. (2006) *History in Practice*, Hodder Arnold.

Levack, B. (3rd edn, 2006) *The Witch-Hunt in Early Modern Europe*, Longman.

Marwick, A. (1970) *The Nature of History*, Macmillan.

Pleuger, G. (1992) 'Chance in history', *History Review*, March.

Sayer, K. (1994), 'Feminism and History', in *Modern History Review*, November.

Stone, L. (1981), *The Past and the Present*, Routledge & Kegan Paul.

Tosh, J. (1984) *The Pursuit of History*, Longman.

Chapter 2

Black, J. and MacRaild, D. (2000) *Studying History*, Macmillan.

Cazorla-Sánchez, A. (2008) 'The New Cultural History – and you' in *History Review*, March)

Evans, R. J. (1998), 'Postmodernism and the study of history' in *History Review*, December.

Green, A. and Troup, K. (1999) *The Houses of History*, Manchester University Press.

Marwick, A. (1970) *The Nature of History*, Macmillan.

Sharpe, J. (2001) *Witchcraft in Early Modern England*, Pearson Education.

Stern, F. (ed.) (1956; 1970) *The Varieties of History*, Meridian Books.

Tosh, J. (1984) *The Pursuit of History*, Longman.

Chapter 3

Adamthwaite, A. (1977) *The Making of the Second World War,* Allen & Unwin.

Barlow, F. (1985) *The Feudal Kingdom of England, 1042–1216*, Longman.

Barrow, G. W. S. (1985) *Feudal Britain*, Edward Arnold.

Brooke, C. (1965) *From Alfred to Henry III*, Nelson.

Butler, Lord (ed.) (1977) *The Conservatives: A History of their Origins to 1965*, Allen & Unwin.

Cain, P. J. and Hopkins, A. G. (1993) *British Imperialism: Innovation and Expansion 1788–1914*, Longman.

Clanchy, M. T. (1988) *England and its Rulers, 1066–1271*, Fontana.

Dickinson, W. C. and Donaldson, G. (eds) (1961) *A Source Book of Scottish History*, vol. III (1567–1707), Thomas Nelson.

Daniels, C. W. and Morrill, J. (1991) *Charles I*, Cambridge University Press.

Eley, G. and Hunt, W. (eds) (1988), *Reviving the English Revolution*, Verso Books.

Everitt, A. (1966) *The Community of Kent and the Great Rebellion,* Leicester University Press.

Feiling, K. (1946) *The Life of Neville Chamberlain*, Macmillan.

Gardiner, S. R. (1902) *Constitutional Documents of the Puritan Revolution*, Oxford University Press.

Henig, R. 'Appeasement and the Origins of the Second World War', in *Perspectives*.

Hill, C. (1961) *The Century of Revolution, 1603–1714*, Sphere.

Hirst, D. (1990) *Authority and Conflict: England 1603–1658*, Edward Arnold.

Hobsbawm, E. J. (1971) *Industry and Empire,* Pelican/Penguin.

Kenyon, J. P. (1985) *Stuart England*, Cambridge University Press.

Loyn, H. R. (1967) *The Norman Conquest*, Hutchinson.

McDonough, F. (1994) The British Empire, 1814–1914, Hodder Murray.

Overy, R. (1994) *The Inter-War Crisis, 1919–1939*, Longman.

Purser, T. (2004) *Medieval England 1042–1228*, Heinemann.

Russell, C. (1984) 'The British Revolution and the English Civil War', professorial inaugural lecture, University College London.

Russell, C. (1991) *The Origins of the English Civil War,* Macmillan.

Sayles, G. O. (1967) *The Medieval Foundations of England*, Methuen.

Smith, S. C. (1998), *British Imperialism 1750–1970* (Cambridge Perspectives in History), Cambridge University Press.

Chapter 4

Brogan, H. (1985) *History of the United States of America*, Longman.

Browning, C. (2005) *The Origins of the Final Solution*, Arrow Books.

Cooke, A. (1977) *Alistair Cooke's America*, BBC Books.

Culpin, C. and Henig, R. (1997) *Modern Europe 1870–1945,* Longman.

Edwardes, C. (17 January 1974) 'Ridley Scott's new Crusades film "panders to Osama bin Laden"', Telegraph.co.uk.

Farmer, A. (1998) *Anti-Semitism and the Holocaust,* Hodder Murray.

Fisher, H. A. L. (1935) A History of Europe, vol. 1, Eyre and Spottiswoode.

Gabrieli, F. (1989) *Arab Historians of the Crusades,* Dorset Press.

Goldhagen, D. (1996) *Hitler's Willing Executioners: Ordinary Germans and the Holocaust*, Little, Brown Book Group.

Hine, R. V. and Faragher, J. M. (2000) *The American West: A New Interpretive History,* Yale University Press.

Hutton, R. 'Counting the Witch Hunt', unpublished essay.

Internet Medieval Sourcebook, Fordham University Center for Medieval Studies.

Kutty, F. (15 July 1999) *Revisiting the Crusades*.

Lavender, D. (1963) *Westward Vision: the Story of the Oregon Trail*, University of Nebraska Press.

Levack, B. (2004) *The Witchcraft Sourcebook,* Routledge.

Levack, B. (2006)*The Witch-hunt in Early Modern Europe,* Pearson Education.

Llewellyn Barstow, A. (1995) *Witchcraze: New History of the European Witch Hunts,* HarperCollins.

McLynn, F. (2003) *Wagons West*, Pimlico.

Phillips, J. (2007) 'Crusade superheroes', in *BBC History Magazine,* vol. 8(8), August.

Rees, L. (2005) *Auschwitz – the Nazis and the Final Solution*, BBC Books.

Riley-Smith, J. (1975) *What were the Crusades?*, Macmillan.

Scarre, G. and Callow, J. (2nd edn, 2001) *Witchcraft and Magic in Sixteenth- and Seventeenth-Century Europe,* Palgrave.

Scribner, R. (1990) 'Witchcraft and judgement in Reformation Germany', in *History Today*, April, pp. 13–4.

Smith, L. (2006) *Forgotten Voices of the Holocaust,* Random House.

Treaty with the New York Indians, Buffalo Creek, New York, 15 January 1838, in 'From Revolution to Reconstruction', Department of Alfa-Informatica, University of Groningen.

Tyerman, C. (2004) *The Crusades: A Very Short Introduction*, Oxford University Press.

Tyerman, C. (2006) *God's War*, Penguin.

United States Holocaust Memorial Museum, 'Wannsee Conference and the "Final Solution"', *Holocaust Encyclopedia*.

Glossary

Analytical history – A method of writing History which is more concerned with explaining events in the past and the relative importance of causes or trends, than with 'telling the story'.

Bottom-up approach – Focuses on ordinary people and their experiences, organisations and actions – as a counter to 'top-down' approaches, which are written from the point of view of those who benefit from historical changes and developments. Tends to see social and economic issues and the local situation in individual towns and villages as very important.

Constructing the past – The way historians constantly develop and write new histories of a particular period or issue, by building on previous interpretations, using new evidence, materials and techniques, and creating new interpretations. The tendency is to see History as being a collection of changing views of the past, and responses to these previous interpretations, rather than the 'actual' past, or even as just 'historiography'.

Continuity – Focuses on the relative impact of certain historical events/developments and the degree of change or continuity with past practices/situations. Assessments of relative change/continuity can be affected by whether a top-down or bottom-up approach is adopted.

Empirical – Focuses on reconstructing the past, and assessing other interpretations, via a study and use of the evidence/facts, rather than taking a theoretical approach.

Factors – Aspects that influence/determine decision-making and historical developments/events, e.g. gender, social, economic, political, religious, etc.

Historical context – What was happening, or what was/was not known at the time/period the source was written/produced, e.g. were certain documents not available when an historian was writing? Was a writer's, or a historian's, view coloured by a significant contemporary event?

Human agency – Stresses the significance of the role of individuals in explaining historical change and developments, i.e. individuals are seen as having choices, and as making conscious decisions. Such interpretations tend to conflict with structural and Marxist approaches.

Indigenous peoples – Local inhabitants already living in a place before outsiders arrived. Especially relevant to studies of British imperialism, the Crusades and the American Wests.

Intentionalist – Focuses on human agency and the role of individuals in historical events, i.e. that such developments were deliberately *intended by an individual leader*.

Interpretation – A particular account or explanation of a period or issue in History, often different from previous accounts or explanations. Some historians argue that it is difficult to arrive at an objective 'truth' – the best that can be achieved is a series of differing interpretations.

Marxist – Historians/historical interpretations that see economic structures and developments as being the main determining (objective) factors behind historical developments and changes. Such approaches/methods are based on the ideas of Karl Marx (d.1883), who stressed the significance of class struggles in such changes; though he did not see history unfolding in a pre-determined/inevitable way, some cruder variations did. Marxist historians also see human agency (subjective factors) as playing a role, but this is considered to be less important than the objective factors.

Methodology – The methods used by historians which contribute to and shape the historical interpretations they produce. These methods may be based on a scientific methodology (such as forming a hypothesis and then testing it against the evidence, and trying to establish certain causal 'laws') in order to establish the truth of the past, or on a close study of primary sources in different regions to see whether experiences varied significantly from place to place.

Motives – Reasons/interests which are seen as explaining why people took certain decisions/actions in the past, e.g. economic, political, social, religious, ambition, etc.

Narrative history – A method of writing History which is concerned to describe the main and most critical developments in a chronological way, so that an overall picture of the past can emerge.

Orthodox – Older interpretations of historical events and developments, which tend to become established until challenged by newer, alternative interpretations or approaches.

Reconstructing the past – The way historians attempt to re-create what the past was like, by basing themselves on the surviving evidence; or by focusing on the 'mentalities' of people in the past, possibly using aspects of sociology, anthropology or psychology.

Revisionist – Newer historical interpretations, which tend – often on the basis of new evidence – to challenge or refine earlier traditional or orthodox interpretations.

Structuralist/functionalist – Explains historical developments by reference to a state's/party's organisation (*structures*), or the economic and social conditions operating at the time, i.e. developments/actions as a *function* of such circumstances/structures.

Synthesis – Interpretation/approach/method that combines elements of earlier, sometimes opposed, interpretations, in order to arrive at a new interpretation.

Thesis – An explanation/interpretation put forward by an historian when attempting to explain why certain developments/changes took place. Actually an hypothesis and tentative, needing further research and confirmation.

Top-down approach – Focuses on central developments and decisions, and those with power and influence, i.e. 'History from above'. Tends to see politics as very important, and contrasts with 'bottom-up' approaches.

Whig approach – Developed in the nineteenth century. Tended to 'read' History backwards from the present, i.e. based on a belief that the 'past was working to the present'. Such an approach was developed by Victorian historians on, for instance, the Norman Conquest and on Britain's seventeenth-century crises. Tends to focus on political or constitutional developments, and to see History 'progressing' to the present.

Index